Crazy Crimes

D1222899

Rupert Matthews

Crazy Crimes

Illustrated by Stuart Trotter

Piccolo Books

First published 1990 by
Pan Books Ltd, Cavaye Place, London SW10 9PG

9 8 7 6 5 4

© Rupert Matthews 1990
ISBN 0 330 31061 5

Phototypeset by Input Typesetting Ltd., London

Printed in England by Clays Ltd, St Ives plc

Introduction

Crooks, like policemen and judges, are just as prone to making mistakes or achieving brilliant success as anyone else. Some criminals are so bad that they manage to guarantee their own capture, others regularly pull off the most amazing stunts. Likewise, some policemen are able to catch their victims by the most incredible tricks.

Perhaps the most interesting type of criminal is the confidence trickster. Some rely on simple tricks to swindle people out of money. Others devise very complex schemes to achieve their purpose. It takes equal cunning to see through the conman and to catch him. Other crooks use very different ways to make money. They might try to burgle ridiculous places: one crook even tried to break into Scotland Yard, the famous headquarters of the London police force.

Crooks are nearly always caught in the end, no matter how clever and successful they are. The tricks and schemes thought up by the police to catch them are every bit as cunning and complex as their own.

This book gathers together some of the most amusing, amazing and astounding cases in the recent history of world crime. Some are so ridiculous as to be almost unbelievable, others are astoundingly elaborate. Perhaps most surprising of all is the fact that they are all true!

Bungled Burglaries

Jan Tomisc was not a happy man. His career as a professional burglar was not going very well and he was becoming desperate. None of the houses he had robbed in recent weeks had contained anything worth stealing; one had even been guarded by a ferocious dog from which Jan had narrowly escaped. As he strolled through the streets of Warsaw in Poland, Jan decided to undertake his biggest robbery yet. His target would be one of the large houses on Boleslav Street.

That night Jan crept into the garden of a luxurious house. He grinned with joy when he found an unlocked window and quietly slipped in. His pocket torch soon revealed that his luck was in, for the beam of light picked up the glint of silver on a sideboard. Lots of silver. Greedily, he opened out his sack and reached forwards for a glittering tray. But then footsteps echoed into the room from a corridor outside, Jan barely had time to dive behind a sofa before two men entered, and one switched on the lights.

'Now we're alone, let's hear what you've got.' said the first man.

'All right.' replied the second. Jan recognised the voice instantly. It belonged to Jaraslav, one of Poland's greatest comics, a man who did impressions of leading politicians and public figures. It soon became clear that he was showing the first man a new show he had worked out.

First, Jaraslav pùt on the voice of the Prime Minister and talked about the failings of the government. The speech was so like that of the real politician, that Jan could not help chuckling to himself. He was getting a free show. Then Jaraslav changed to the voice of the Home Secretary, a man Jan could not stand. The jokes were so funny that he began to rock with silent laughter, yet he knew he dare not make a noise in case he was heard.

When Jaraslav moved on the the Bishop of Cracow, Jan had to stuff a handkerchief in his mouth in a desperate attempt to keep quiet. Tears were running down his cheeks and he felt that he was about to burst. The jokes continued to come flying thick and fast, and Jan became so convulsed with mirth that he did not notice the handkerchief working loose. Suddenly it dropped from his mouth and he exploded into guffaws of laughter. Jaraslav stopped his performance and ran to phone the police. Jan was still doubled over with laughter when he was dragged out to the waiting police car.

Many burglars have been caught in similarly unlucky circumstances, among them Billy Brady. But Brady had only himself to blame for being captured. His crime took place in Hove, in September 1922.

He crept across the dark garden of one of the large Georgian houses in Lansdowne Avenue. It was well past midnight, but he wanted to be certain that everybody was asleep. Reaching a window on the ground floor, he waited in the darkness. He could hear nothing from inside the house, and no lights were showing. Guessing that everybody was asleep, Billy levered the window open and sprang inside.

He found himself in a large stone-flagged room. Carefully flashing his torch around, he realised that he was in the kitchen. He crept across the room to a door which evidently led into the rest of the house. It was locked.

For some minutes he tried to pick the lock, but he could not manage it. Finally putting his lock pick down, he crept back to the window. He looked outside, but no other windows were within reach of the ground.

Disappointed at not being able to reach other parts of the house, Billy decided to search the kitchen. Perhaps he would be able to find something worth stealing there. He crept to a long sideboard and carefully opened the drawers, hoping to find silver cutlery. Instead, they were filled with old spoons and teatowels. Next he tried a cupboard, and here he found something much more interesting: food.

The shelves of the cupboard were packed with foods of every kind imaginable and Billy was hungry. Checking that nobody had heard him, he reached out for a tempting pork pie. Cutting himself a generous slice, he sat down at the kitchen table to eat. After a mouthful or two it occurred to him that he would like some pickles and he went back to the cupboard for some.

After polishing off his pie and pickles, Billy noticed some ham. He made himself a ham sandwich and gulped this down. Next he spotted a cold chicken, and cut himself some slices for a second sandwich. A large sherry trifle then took his fancy and he quickly downed a bowlful before returning to the cupboard for a slice of some chocolate cake he had noticed.

Having finished off the cake, he felt absolutely full. He leaned back in the chair, closed his eyes and fell fast asleep.

As dawn broke, the cook came downstairs to start getting breakfast ready. She unlocked the kitchen door and walked in to see Billy fast asleep at the table surrounded by empty plates and crumbs. Realising immediately what had happened, she turned around and ran outside to call the police.

Billy was still asleep when two burly policemen pounced on him and dragged him off to prison.

Pierre LeBlanc was not as careless as Billy Brady, but he was caught nonetheless. In fact Pierre was so careful not to leave any evidence behind him at the houses he burgled that the police in Paris almost gave up trying to convict him. They knew that Pierre was a burglar, but they never had enough evidence to sustain a prosecution.

Then Inspector Jardin had an idea. One morning, he arrived at his police station looking very pleased with himself.

'You're looking very happy,' commented Superintendant Artois, 'Have you won some money on the horses?'

'No, chief,' replied Jardin. 'I've worked out how to convict LeBlanc.'

'How?' gasped Artois. 'Have you found some evidence?'

'Oh no,' smiled Jardin 'I don't need evidence. Just your permission to arrest him next time there's a burglary we think he committed.'

Artois was puzzled, but Jardin would not reveal his plan. Finally Artois gave his permission for the unusual act of arresting a man without evidence. 'But remember,' he said, 'without evidence you can only hold a man for twenty-four hours.' Jardin just grinned.

A fortnight later a house was burgled, and the crime showed all the hallmarks of a job by LeBlanc. Only jewellery had been stolen and no clues had been left behind. Jardin immediately called on LeBlanc and arrested him. He was taken to the police station and put in a cell. Jardin spent some hours questioning him, but the crook could not be caught out. He claimed he had spent the entire evening sitting at home reading a book.

When the questioning was over, Jardin came out smiling.

'Well' asked Artois, 'did you get your evidence?'

'No' he replied 'But I shall.'

He spent the rest of the day at the scene of the crime. He discovered where the burglar had broken in, which desks and cupboards he had opened, and exactly what he had stolen. He went back to the police station and wrote all the information out. Then he sat down to wait. Artois, fascinated to see what he was up to, waited with him.

At about three o'clock in the morning, Jardin finally stood up.

'Come on, Chief,' he said. 'It's time to convict LeBlanc.'

The two detectives entered the cell where LeBlanc was sleeping. They sat down on the stools, Jardin holding his notebook open in front of him.

'Wake up,' called Jardin.

LeBlanc opened his eyes rather sleepily, 'What is it?' he asked.

'You've been talking in your sleep,' said Jardin. 'Listen to this.' He then read out his own account of how the burglary had been carried out the previous night. When he had finished, he set the pad down and turned to LeBlanc. 'That's how you did it isn't it?'

'Yes,' replied the thief sleepily, before he had time to realise what he was saying. The confession was good enough to convict him.

Marcel Gauf, caught by Inspector Jardin a few years later, could only blame himself for his capture.

Called to the scene of a burglary in the middle of the night by a worried householder, Jardin arrived accompanied by two uniformed officers.

'What has been stolen?' Jardin asked.

'All my silver cutlery, and a pair of silver candle-sticks,' replied the man, 'They were taken from the lounge.'

One of the first things Jardin spotted when he entered the lounge was a small book lying on the floor.

'Is this yours?' he asked the householder.

The man looked at the small blue book, then replied that he had never seen it before.

Jardin opened it. At the front was an inscription reading; 'This book belongs to Marcel Gauf, 24 rue Antoine, Paris.'

'Come on,' ordered Jardin to his men. He led them outside and into a police car which he hurriedly drove to the rue Antoine. He pulled up just as Gauf was returning home with a sack containing the silver candlesticks and cutlery. He was arrested on the spot.

Thomas Smith was a burglar who specialised in breaking into guest houses in seaside resorts in southern England. He knew that people on holiday often carry large amounts of cash. While his victims slept, he would go through their pockets, taking anything he fancied. His career came to an end when he tried to rob a guest house in Bognor Regis.

At first, everything seemed to be going well. Smith clambered over the back garden wall without being seen and crept up to the rear of the house. For a few moments he listened to make sure that nobody was moving around in the house. Then he tried the windows on the ground floor. They were all locked.

Glancing up, Smith saw that one of the windows on the first floor was open. Climbing up a convenient drainpipe, he clambered in through the window and found himself in a bedroom containing two beds. Moonlight streamed in from outside, illuminating the whole scene.

He could see enough without his torch, so he slipped it back into his pocket. Nobody was sleeping in the room, so he was not as careful as usual about being silent. He began going through the drawers. They were filled with dresses and skirts, but no money.

Then he heard the front door open and close, followed by the sound of footsteps on the stairs. Fearing that he might be discovered, Smith dived beneath one of the beds. Sure enough the light in the room was switched on and Smith saw two pairs of feet enter both wearing high-heeled shoes.

One of them stepped over to the bed where Smith was hiding and flopped down. The bottom of the bed bulged downwards, smacking him on the head.

'Phew,' gasped the woman, 'My feet are killing me.'

'I'm not surprised, Mary,' replied the other one, 'with the amount of dancing you've done this evening, and most of it with that dark-haired boy.'

'Peter, you mean?' queried Mary, 'He's quite nice. Anyway you're one to talk, Helen Daniels. You were making eyes at that blond boy.'

'Me?' exclaimed Helen, 'I like that!'

Smith remained motionless under the bed. He hoped that the girls would soon go to sleep so that he could sneak out. He waited while they changed into their nightdresses and climbed into bed. After some minutes chatting about the dance they switched off the lights.

He waited a few minutes to give them time to fall asleep, then began edging his way out from the bed.

'Mary, how about going round the shops tomorrow?' asked Helen.

He froze and inched his way back into hiding, lying still and listening to the girls discussing whether or not to go shopping for new clothes the following morning.

Finally they fell silent again. Smith was just about to leave when Helen spoke again.

'Its such a shame we have to go back on Sunday,' she said. 'I'll be back at work this time next week.'

'Well at least you don't work for that horrid Mr Bennet in accounts,' replied her friend.

Once again, the intruder had to wait motionless while the girls chatted, this time about the office where they worked. Suddenly a terrible cramp gripped

Smith's leg. He was not used to remaining still in a small space for so long. The cramp spread, becoming increasingly painful.

The girls fell silent again. Soon Smith was relieved to hear the sound of steady breathing which showed him they were asleep.

Slowly and carefully, he wriggled out from his tiny hiding place, then glanced at his watch in the moonlight and was amazed to see that he had been trapped for nearly three hours.

He quickly stood up but he had forgotten his cramp which returned with agonising pain, making him stagger forwards. Crashing into a table, he fell to the ground scattering perfume bottles noisily on the floor. The girls woke up screaming as he scrambled to his feet and dashed for the window. He was too late; a man sleeping in the next room rushed in, saw Smith and pounced. Within seconds a policeman had arrived and he hauled Smith off to prison, muttering about the girls' dull conversation as he was dragged away.

In 1981 the career of William Thomas came to a sudden end when he decided to rob a jeweller's shop in Brighton. He knew where to dispose of any loot he might take, at a good price. All he had to do was get hold of the jewels.

Leaving his car parked down a sidestreet, he strode up to the jeweller's window. Glancing around to check that nobody was close enough to interfere, he pulled a brick from his coat and flung it at the window. The brick bounced back off the toughened glass, struck Thomas on the head and knocked him unconscious. The staff of the shop called a policeman who hauled him straight off to prison.

Another burglar who engineered his own capture was Pete Brown, who attempted to break into Weedon Post Office in Northamptonshire. For some days before his planned raid, Brown waited in Weedon High Street making careful notes of who was in the building at what times and how the building was locked up at night. It soon became clear that the cash box was only unguarded at night. Unfortunately the post office was secured each evening with locks too difficult for Brown to pick.

Then he noticed a weakness. The roof above the cash room was flat and built of timber. All he had to do was to climb on to the roof and saw his way through it.

On the Saturday night he had chosen for the raid, Brown scrambled up onto the roof armed with a large saw, and started work in the pale moonlight. He quickly hacked his way through the timbers.

In less than half an hour a neat circular hole had been cut in the roof, through which Brown dropped the bag in which he intended to place his loot, then lowered himself.

He was about halfway through when he realised that his belt was caught on a projecting piece of timber. Realising he would have to cut the wood before he could get through, he began to push himself out. He then found that he was truly stuck and unable to move. The more he struggled, the tighter he became stuck. In the end he gave up the struggle and relaxed.

At six the next morning the postmaster unlocked the front door and was surprised to see a bag in the middle of the floor and a pair of legs dangling through the ceiling! The thief was arrested immediately.

In 1922, a thief attempted to rob an antique shop in Paris belonging to Monsieur Tiercellette. At first everything went well. He broke into the shop without being spotted by anybody and began searching it for valuables. Before long he had amassed a sizeable collection of silver and jewellery which he had stowed away in a bag.

Then he saw Monsieur Tiercellette strolling towards the shop. The only way out was through the front door, and that would mean he would be spotted by the owner. He looked around for a hiding place, but saw nowhere suitable. He heard the key in the lock. The owner was about to enter.

Suddenly, he had what at the time seemed a good idea. He spotted a suit of armour standing in the corner of the shop. Hurriedly stepping behind it, he put on the helmet and breastplace. He hoped to frighten Monsieur Tiercellette by pretending to be a ghost.

When Tiercellette entered, he lumbered forwards in the dark making hideous ghostly, groaning noises.

Far from running, however, Tiercellette switched on the lights, the crook tripped over and fell headlong onto the floor with a resounding crash, whereupon the owner piled chairs on top of him and called the police.

Some burglaries are bungled not by the burglar but by the policeman trying to catch him. Perhaps the best known such incident occured in the South Riding of Yorkshire.

The story began in 1922 when young PC Roberts, new to the night beat, was patrolling a wealthy street. He had been asked to keep a special eye on No. 45

as the owners were away on holiday. Such requests were not unusual, but as the owner was a local judge, Roberts was told to keep a special watch on the place, as it was feared that local crooks might raid the house in revenge for the judge's stiff sentences.

As Roberts strolled along the street he saw a flash of light from No. 45. He stopped and watched. Somebody was moving around in the house using a torch. Thinking that a burglar was at work, he crept up to the house.

He soon found an open window, clearly the route by which the burglar had entered, so he slipped in and cautiously made his way through the house. Hearing the sound of footsteps overhead, he quietly climbed the stairs.

As he reached the top. Roberts saw the torch coming along the landing. He pushed himself into a doorway and waited for the burglar. When the man drew level, Roberts pounced, throwing him to the floor. The intruder punched Roberts in the stomach and the policeman struck back, winding him completely.

Groping in the dark, he handcuffed the man and then switched on his own torch. He was horrified to find himself staring into the face of the judge, who had returned a few days early.

He was far from satisfied. He complained to the police authorities and threatened to sue Roberts for assult. He said that the constable should have checked to see if the man wandering through the house really was a burglar before trying to arrest him. At one point it seemed as if he would lose his job, but the fuss died down in time.

Three years later Roberts was patrolling the same street at night. Again he saw a figure moving through the house with a torch. Remembering that the judge had said he often used a torch to avoid awaking his family if he wanted to get up in the night, Roberts decided to wait before approaching the house. He watched as the torch continued to roam the house, then decided to investigate.

Rather than enter the house, he marched up to the front door and rang the bell. He heard footsteps, followed by a loud scream, some shouting and then more footsteps. As soon as the door opened, he rushed in to find the judge and his wife staring at him angrily.

'What did you ring the bell for, you fool,' bellowed the judge. 'There was a burglar in here. When you rang you woke us up and he ran for it. Why didn't you come in after him and arrest him?'

Roberts sighed. You just can't please some people, he thought.

Conmen and Frauds

Conmen make money by tricking people. Some of them are very good actors, but even the best can be caught by the simplest of tricks. While they know that they are acting, the pretence is superb, but once they relax they can be caught out. It was in this way that a crook was convicted of shoplifting at Willesden Crown Court in London in 1913.

The woman who had been arrested said that she was a foreigner who spoke hardly any English and had not been able to read the signs in the shop. Throughout the short hearing, she spoke in extremely bad English with a very strong accent. She managed to convince everyone that she was, indeed, a foreigner.

Judge Parfitt, however, was not so sure. He studied the woman through his glasses while the store detective gave evidence against her. It seemed to him that she was listening to what was being said, although she pretended to be unable to speak English properly.

The more he watched, the more convinced he was that she was tricking the court. He decided to trick her in return.

As the store detective finished his evidence, the Judge beckoned the Clerk to his desk.

'I think we should break for lunch now,' he said.

The Clerk glanced at the clock. 'Very good, my lord,' he said. 'Shall we reconvene at two?' Parfitt nodded. The clerk turned to the court. 'The court shall now rise and reconvene at two o'clock,' he said.

Judge Parfitt rose from his chair as the lawyer and the woman defendant got up to leave. Rather than leave by the rear door of the court, he made as if to leave by the front door. When he came up behind the woman, he tapped her on the shoulder.

'Could you lend me five pounds?' he asked.

Without thinking she turned round. 'A fiver!' she exclaimed. 'You're joking!'

Only then did she realise that she had been caught out. When the court met again in the afternoon, her defence was abandoned and she was found guilty as charged.

Detective Sergeant Wilson was nearly taken in by a conman in Liverpool. He was idly flicking through his local newspaper when he came across an advertisement which read: *Gentleman leaving for Italy on business must dispose of all furniture.*

The advertisement was followed by a phone number.

As it happened Wilson had recently moved into a larger home and needed some pieces of furniture. Thinking that he might be able to pick up some cheap items, he called the number and arranged to make a visit.

The following day he found himself outside a flat in a smart area of town. He rang the doorbell. Seconds later the door opened and he was greeted by a smartly dressed young man.

'Good evening,' said Wilson. 'I called about seeing your furniture.'

'Oh, yes,' said the man. 'You must be Mr Wilson. My name's Jackson.'

The two men shook hands and Wilson stepped into the flat and looked around. There was certainly some very fine furniture there.

'Did you want anything in particular?'

'I was after some lounge chairs,' said Wilson, 'and some sidetables.'

'Oh I've got those,' said Jackson with a winning smile. 'It's such a shame I've got to go to Italy, but the firm is paying all expenses.'

They went into the lounge of the flat, and Wilson stopped dead in surprise.

In front of him was an antique dining table and chairs which had been reported to him as stolen just two days earlier. Recovering from his surprise, he inspected the chairs. They were fine pieces, and the price was very low.

He knew that something was wrong, but pretended to be interested in the chairs and arranged to call back later with a van to take them away. He left the flat and hurried round to his police station. There he told the desk sergeant about the stolen antiques and took a force of men round to the flat.

Bursting in, they arrested Jackson and took the furniture under guard. It later proved that he had been pretending to leave for Italy for over eight months. In reality he was acting as a 'fence' to sell stolen property for various local crooks. He had been conning people into believing his story as a cover for the illegal sales.

Victor Lustig was a Czech national who moved to France after the First World War. He was tall, good-looking and always wore the smartest and most fashionable clothes. He appeared to be a respectable and honourable businessman.

In the summer of 1925 Lustig read a report in the newspaper *Le Figaro* that the Eiffel Tower, the famous Parisian landmark, was in desperate need of repairs. The report added that the repairs were likely to be extremely expensive and that it had even been suggested that the cost was too much and that the tower should be demolished.

He saw the opportunity for the greatest con trick of his life, and got together with a colleague of his, a fellow conman called Pierre, and hatched a plot.

First he had some headed notepaper printed bearing the title of a government department. Then he sent letters to five major metalworks asking them to send representatives to meet him at a hotel. Lustig described himself as Director in Charge of the Eiffel Tower.

The five representatives arrived at the hotel suite he had hired for the purpose. Two of them seemed the most eager to do business with the government.

'Gentlemen,' he began, speaking with the carefully pronounced accent of a senior civil servant. 'I have asked you here to discuss a very delicate matter. As you know the Eiffel Tower is in need of repairs. Unfortunately, the cost is so high that the government is unable to meet it. It has therefore been decided to sell the tower for scrap.'

There was a gasp of astonishment from the metal dealers.

'We realise that this will cause a public outcry. That is why we have to hold these meetings away from the ministry. The public must not learn what is happening until the deal has been finalised and demolition work has begun. Then it will be too late for the public to do anything.'

He cast his eye kindly at the men listening to him.

'The government has invited you five gentlemen to submit bids for the scrap metal as we know you to be both skilled and discreet. Secrecy is essential.'

'Are you serious about this?' asked Lafitte, one of the dealers.

'Of course,' replied Lustig. 'It is very sad, but we have no choice.'

'How much scrap is involved?' asked another, called Pruit.

'About seven thousand tonnes,' said Lustig. 'It is a big structure.'

The metal dealers nodded their agreement.

'Very well,' said Lustig. 'You now know the proposal. You would be responsible for the demolition, of course, and you would keep all the metal in the tower. I would like you to send your written bids for the contract to me here within five days.'

With that Lustig ushered his victims from the door. After they had gone he turned to his colleague.

'Do you think they'll go for it?' he asked.

'Of course,' said Pierre. 'That Pruit looked so greedy. He thinks he can make a fat profit from this. He'll put in a good bid.'

'What about Lafitte?' asked Lustig.

'I'm not sure,' said Pierre. 'He might go for it. The others won't submit bids. They didn't look interested. We'll have to be careful though, one of them might contact the government to see if the offer is genuine.'

Lustig shrugged. 'We'll just have to take our chance.'

When the five days were up the swindlers had received the two bids they expected from Lafitte and Pruit. The others had not taken the bait.

'Lafitte has offered more money, but I think we should go for Pruit,' said Pierre. 'He's so greedy he'll believe anything we tell him if he sees a profit in it.'

'Agreed. Write him a letter saying we've accepted his bid and get him to bring a cheque for a tenth of the amount as a deposit.'

'Why not ask for a quarter?' suggested Pierre. 'I'm certain he'll fall for it.'

'All right, make it a quarter.'

Three days later Pruit arrived at the hotel suite with a cheque for several hundred thousand francs in his pocket. He eagerly handed the cheque over in return for official-looking documents assigning him ownership of the Eiffel Tower and giving him permission to pull it down for scrap. Pruit pocketed the documents and hurried back to his firm to make arrangements for work to begin.

Lustig and Pierre waited until he left, then hurriedly packed their bags, cashed the cheque and left for the USA with a fortune in their pockets. Lustig remained free for some years, practising as a confidence trickster, but he never again pulled off such a spectacular stunt as selling the Eiffel Tower. Justice eventually caught up with him when he became involved with forging banknotes.

One of the shortest and most rewarding cons, in terms of money per minute, was invented by a man named Wilson Mitzner in 1921 when he spotted a short man with big feet in Atlantic City, New Jersey, one day.

'Excuse me,' he said. 'I hope you don't mind my stopping you like this, but how would you like to earn some quick money?'

'I'd love to,' said the man, 'I've been unemployed for several weeks now, and the rent on my house is overdue. What do you want me to do? I'm an accountant by profession.'

'Oh, it's not work,' said Mizner. 'It's a sort of trick.'

'Trick? What do you mean?'

'Come down to the beach with me. I'll show you.'

The two strolled off and the short man introduced himself as Jonathan Adams.

'Now then, Jonathan,' said Mizner when they reached the beach. 'All I want you to do is sit down behind this windbreak and stick your feet out underneath it.'

'Is that it?' asked Adams.

'It certainly is. Just leave the rest to me.'

Not entirely sure what was happening, but hoping to make some money out of it, he sat down and stuck his feet out into view.

Mizner walked off and hung around on the beach a few yards away. Before long he saw a man walking towards him. He set off so he would meet the man right beside the windbreak. When they drew close, Mizner suddenly stopped as if in surprise.

'Well, bless my soul,' he exclaimed.

'What is it?' asked the man.

'Why, look at those feet,' said Mizner pointing at Adams' legs. 'They're enormous!'

'They sure are,' replied the man.

27

'How tall do you reckon this chap is?'

He put his head on one side as he thought.

'I'd reckon on about six feet or so.'

'Never,' said Mizner. 'I reckon he's under six feet.'

'Come off it! A man with such big feet must be taller than that.'

'Tell you what,' said Mizner, smiling in his most charming manner, 'why not bet a dollar on whether the man is over six feet or not?'

'OK,' said the passer-by, thinking that he was sure to win.

They walked over to the screen and Mizner pretended to be very surprised when Adams turned out to be just five feet two inches tall. The man paid his dollar and wondered off, not realising he had been cheated.

All day long the crooked betting continued. Each time he stopped someone, Mizner would guess at a slightly lower height than the passer-by. He won every time.

Only when a passing policeman began watching him did he stop the confidence trick. Handing Adams half the day's takings, he strolled off and remained free until he was caught for a racecourse con trick several years later.

Marcel Lefoivre was robbed of a large amount of money by a more complicated trick. One morning in 1922 he received a visitor at his new house. 'I'm sorry to trouble you like this,' he said after he had been shown in. 'But I have a proposal to put to you.'

'What is it?' asked Lefoivre.

'Well, my name is Leclare and before the War this house was owned by an elderly aunt of mine. I have

just learnt that before she died she hid a lot of money in a chest and buried it in the garden.'

'Oh yes?' Lefoivre was becoming interested.

'The problem is that you now own the garden. Since my aunt didn't make a will the money now belongs to you.'

Lefoivre had visions of being rich.

'However,' continued Leclare, 'you do not know where the money is and I do. I suggest that we make a deal. I'll show you where the box is and we'll split whatever's inside it.'

Lefoivre thought about the idea for a few minutes. He could see nothing wrong with the idea. The house had a large garden. He might never find the box without Leclare's help.

'All right,' he said. 'I'll fetch a shovel.'

Minutes later the two men were in the garden.

'It's by this tree,' said Leclare, pointing at a gnarled apple tree. He marched over, stood with his back to it and then took five paces towards the house. 'Here,' he said and began digging.

At a depth of around a metre Leclare uncovered an old wooden box. It turned out to be filled with silver franc pieces. Lefoivre gazed at them greedily.

'I'll tell you what,' said Leclare. 'Rather than having me carry all these coins away, why don't you just give me a cheque for half the amount.' He looked at the box. 'I'd guess there are ten thousand francs in there. Give me a cheque for five thousand and we'll be square.'

Lefoivre eyed the box. He estimated that there were far more than ten thousand francs there. By handing over such a small amount he thought he would make a huge profit on the deal. Hurrying back to the house he wrote a cheque and sent Leclare on his way.

Only when he took the coins to a bank did he discover that they were duds, hardly worth a hundred francs altogether. Apparently the man calling himself Leclare had buried similar boxes in gardens all over Paris and had pulled the same trick many times.

A daring trick began with an advert in a German newspaper in 1968. It was read by an Italian businessman named Bruno, who was living in Germany, and stated that an Italian girl was looking for a penpal and gave an address in Naples. Bruno replied to the advert. In return he got a charming letter from a girl named Angela Favoroti and a photograph of an extremely attractive girl.

He hastily replied to the letter and soon a busy correspondence had sprung up between the two. Then Angela suggested that she should visit Bruno, but pointed out that she did not have enough money to make the trip. He happily sent her the cash to pay for her ticket.

After sending the money, he never heard from her again. He had been tricked, but did not let matters rest there. A few months later he went home to Italy to visit his family and while he was there he took a trip to Naples and tracked down the address at which he had been writing to Angela.

As he turned a corner, he was staggered to find himself in front of a prison. He checked the street and the number. There could be no doubt he was at the right address. Perhaps his penpal was a convict!

Hesitatingly, he rang the doorbell.

'Do you have a woman named Angela Favoroti here?' he asked the guard who answered.

He frowned and then consulted a long list.

'No,' he said. 'But we have a man named Angelo Favoroti who is here on robbery charges.'

Hurriedly, Bruno·told his story to the guard who passed it on to the prison governor. It later came out that the prison warders were not allowed to read mail going in and out of the prison, so Angelo Favoroti and some friends had been running the penpal trick for some time.

Charles King was not only ambitious but was also blatantly obvious in his crime and was easily caught out, although by that time he had achieved his aim. In 1928, he was the President of the African nation of Liberia. Following the laws of the land, he had to put himself up for re-election. Using underhand methods of ballot rigging, he won a resounding victory. He beat his nearest rival, Thomas Faulkner, by over 600,000 votes.

Faulkner immediately accused him of cheating. When asked why he thought the president had rigged the election, Faulkner pointed out that only 15,000 Liberians were entitled to vote. Where, he asked, did the remaining 585,000 votes come from?

Unlike Charles King, Marc Colombo did not really intend his trick to be on a very large scale. But almost in spite of himself, he managed to strip his employers of £32 million and to plunge a major international bank into a huge scandal.

Before staring on his haphazard path to disgrace, he was a foreign exchange dealer at the Lloyds Bank in Lugano, Switzerland. His job was to monitor the daily shifts in exchange rates between the currencies of different nations. If he thought he could make money by buying and selling he was allowed to do so, but at no time were his debts allowed to total more than £700,000. He was also supposed to report all his transactions to his boss, Signor Mombelli.

In November 1973, he thought that he saw a way to make a lot of money, but it involved breaking the rules. He decided to go ahead, anyway.

He believed that the American dollar was about to lose value against other currencies and therefore agreed to buy $34 million in three months' time with Swiss francs. If he was right and the dollar fell in value, he would be able to purchase the dollars with fewer francs than expected and would be in profit.

In fact the dollar rose and he had to pay seven million Swiss francs more than expected.

He knew that if he admitted this to Mombelli, he would lose his job, so he decided to try to win back his loss.

He invested $68 million in the hope of recouping as much as possible while still showing a profit. Instead he lost again. He did not inform either his boss or the Swiss credit control system of what he was doing, but simply phoned other banks and agreed deals with them by word of mouth. Banking depends to a large extent on trust and Colombo took advantage of this fact for his trickery.

He decided to gamble again and he continued to do so for several months. Indeed, he might have gone on for several years, because Mombelli did not understand international finance and believed whatever Colombo told him.

However, in August 1974 a banquet was organised in the City of London for the chiefs of various large banks. The head of Lloyds was there, as was the chief of the Clisson Bank in Paris. They were discussing foreign exchange and the Frenchman happened to remark, 'Your Lugano branch has reached its credit limit with us.'

The Lloyds man was staggered. To reach such a limit would involve deals of hundreds of millions of pounds. Yet Lugano had a limit of £700,000. The next morning Lloyds began phoning round other European banks. They were told that the Lugano bank had large debts with all of them.

A team of high-level executives caught the next plane to Lugano, seized all the records of that branch, suspended all trading and dragged Colombo and Mombelli back to London. They found that Colombo had set up deals worth a total of over £4,500 million. More than £235 million worth of these were still outstanding.

The shocked executives of Lloyds spent three weeks tracing all the deals and debts which had run up. They found that they had lost over £32 million in less than a year. They hurriedly paid their debts and prosecuted both Colombo and Mombelli for fraud.

In the court case, which was heard in Switzerland, it soon became obvious that Mombelli was innocent. Colombo had exploited his ignorance and, although he had been foolish, he had not been dishonest. He was released. Colombo, meanwhile, pointed out that apart from his initial gamble of $34 million, he had not been trying to make a profit, but merely cover his losses. He was found guilty, but was only given eighteen months' suspended jail sentence. He had pulled off the biggest fraud in the history of international banking, but walked free because he had not meant it to happen on such a huge scale.

Franz Tausend was greedier; he conned millions out of bankers and businessmen during the 1920s. For years, he had made a living as a petty criminal and conman in Germany. Then he read about medieval alchemists who had tried to turn lead into gold; some of them had been employed by wealthy noblemen for many years.

That was hundreds of years earlier and he wondered if people were still gullible enough to think gold could be made from lead. He decided that they were and set out to prove it.

First he set up an institution with the grand name of the Chemical Research Society. Then he claimed to have accidentally produced gold during an experiment. He approached various people and told them that all he needed was some money to help him recreate the experiment. He said that he would soon discover what had happened and begin producing gold in large quantities.

Amazingly several dozen people believed him. Among them was the level-headed World War I hero, General Ludendorf. They happily handed over many thousands of German marks to help Tausend with his 'experiments'. Of course, he actually conducted no experiments at all, but simply pocketed the cash.

When news got around that he had bought himself a castle worth a small fortune, his investors became suspicious. They reasoned that one of two things had happened. Either he had found the secret of making gold, but had not told them, or he was cheating them. He was then arrested, convicted of fraud and put in prison for four years.

Confidence tricksters rely on two features of human nature. The first is that most people want to make money without much effort. The second is that many of us are willing to trust someone who seems honest. By being both greedy and trusting, many people have been cheated out of money. However, this can work both ways: a person might miss out on making a fortune by being too sceptical and untrusting. A classic instance of this occurred in South Africa in 1866.

Around Christmas, Schalk van Niekerk, the owner of a remote farm near Hopetown, found his son playing marbles with a neighbour's children. The boys were using pebbles which they had picked up nearby. One of the pebbles was clear and bright. Van Niekerk asked his son if he could borrow it. He thought it might be worth some money.

A few months later a merchant named John O'Reilly passed through the village. He was selling farm equipment, cloth and knives; in fact, he would sell anything the farmers wanted to buy. Van Niekerk walked up to him.

'Here,' he said, 'you know about these things. What do you reckon this is?' He held out his shiny pebble.

'To be sure, I don't know,' said O'Reilly. 'But it looks good to me. It could be an opal or a topaz. They've found such stones down by Klipplaat.'

'Are they worth much?'

O'Reilly shrugged. 'A bit,' he said. 'You might be able to buy yourself a new cart with it. Tell you what; I'll take it with me to Colesburg and ask the merchants there.'

'How much would you want for doing that?' asked van Niekerk.

'Say one tenth of what its worth. That way if it's worth nothing you don't owe me anything.'

'Fair enough,' he agreed, and handed the stone over.

Several dys later O'Reilly finished his tour around the remote villages and returned to the town of Colesburg. He showed the pebble to some of his fellow traders, but none of them knew what it was. As a last resort O'Reilly took it to Lorenzo Boyson, the local government commissioner.

He sat at his desk and studied the stone with a magnifying glass, then looked at O'Reilly.

'I don't want to get your hopes up,' he said, 'but I think this is a diamond.'

'A diamond?' gasped O'Reilly. 'But they're worth a fortune!'

'That's right. If this is a diamond it would be worth around £500.'

O'Reilly boggled. At the time this was a huge sum which it would take him over a year to earn as a trader.

'How can we find out if it is a diamond?' he asked.

'I'll send it to a pal of mine who's a jeweller,' said Boyson. 'He'll tell us.'

He sent the diamond to his friend who confirmed that it was a diamond. It was sent on to London. There a businessman by the name of John Curry heard of the find. He tried to get investors to put money into a scheme for starting a diamond mine.

Nobody was interested. They just laughed at him.

'Fancy believing some old trader,' said one man.

'There are no diamonds in South Africa,' said a second. 'You must think we were born yesterday!'

Finally Curry took the diamond to Sir Roderick Murchison, the greatest jewel expert in London. He looked at the jewel then put it aside.

'If you say this diamond was found in Hopetown,' he said, 'then I believe you. But if you ask me to say on the basis of one stone that Hopetown is a diamond-producing area, I must decline.'

When, a few months later, a second diamond arrived in London from Hopetown, Curry was overjoyed. Once again he tried to interest people in his scheme, but again no-one believed him. Finally a diamond mining expert agreed to visit the site to make a study.

He found nothing but open sand. 'Perhaps somebody dropped the stones?' he suggested. 'Or maybe ostriches brought them here.'

Curry was still the laughing stock of London. But when, a few months later, dozens of diamonds were found, he was the one laughing. All the men who had turned him down realised they had missed a fortune because they were just too suspicious!

Courtroom Capers

The courtroom is an impressive place. Most people who appear in court, either accused of a crime or as a witness manage to cope with the situation well, but some suffer from bad attacks of nerves or make simple mistakes which have disastrous consequences.

In 1948 a man named Stephen Comyn was in court accused of shoplifting. The prosecuting lawyer, James Tidy, asked him what his profession was.

'I am a travelling minstrel,' he declared.

'Being a tramp and a busker is not a very dignified job, is it?' asked Tidy pointedly. He hoped to show that Comyn was an untrustworthy man.

'Not particularly,' he replied 'but it's better than what my father did.'

'And what was that?' asked Tidy, expecting him to admit his father was a thief or a crook of some kind.

'He was a lawyer,' he replied with complete seriousness.

The look of surprise on Tidy's face caused the public gallery to collapse with laughter.

Michael Stephens also lost face – and his freedom – by being over-clever in court. He was arrested for snatching a handbag from a woman in Tulsa, Oklahoma, and decided to conduct his own defence, perhaps believing he could make a better job of it than any lawyer.

He was wrong.

He based his defence upon the idea that the victim had wrongly identified him and that it was another similar man who had robbed her. When the victim took the stand, Stephens asked her questions regarding the appearance of the man who had robbed her.

'What colour was his hair?' he asked.

'It was blonde, just like yours,' she replied.

'And how tall was the man?'

'About five foot ten, same as you.'

'Ah,' said Stephens addressing the jury, 'but there are many blond men a little under six feet tall in Tulsa.' He spun round dramatically to face the woman.

'But did you get a good look at my face when I took your bag?' Stephens demanded.

As soon as he realised what he had said, Stephens covered his face with his hands and quietly pleaded guilty.

Rather odd evidence came to light in a burglary case in Southwark Crown Court in London. Culpeper Fry and Norman Chunn were accused of several burglaries over the previous few months. The Clerk of the Court rose to his feet.

'You are accused,' he began, 'of stealing silver worth £2,000 from 27 Palace Road on October 14th. How do you plead?'

'Not guilty,' said Chunn.

'Not guilty,' said Fry.

'You are further charged with stealing jewellery worth £4,000 from 18 Grove Way on October 22nd. How do you plead?'

'Not guilty,' said Fry.

Chunn looked rather puzzled and glanced at his companion in the dock. 'Not guilty,' he said gazing hard at his colleague.

'You are further charged with stealing silver and ornaments worth £6,000 from 32 Westfield Road on November 6th. How do you plead?'

'Not guilty,' said Fry; whereupon Chunn suddenly turned and grabbed him by the throat; cursing him as he did so.

'You swine,' he shouted, 'You told me that stuff was next to worthless. You've been cheating me!'

'Shut up,' hissed Fry. 'You'll give everything away!' But it was too late, Chunn brought his massive fist back and punched so hard that Fry crashed unconscious to the floor.

He turned to face the astonished judge.

'I'd like to change my plea to guilty,' he said. 'And while we're about it I'll tell you a few more things about Fry here.'

While the ushers dragged the injured man out and called a doctor, Chunn proceeded to describe how his one-time friend dealt with other crooks, organising burglaries and disposing of the loot.

When the amazing outburst was over, he was found guilty and given a light sentence. Fry returned to court the next day to be convicted of a long list of extra charges and sent to prison for fifteen years.

Sometimes the evidence of police officers is called into question by defence lawyers. They try to discredit the policeman and so get a verdict of not guilty. In February 1989 a policeman was giving evidence at Richmond Crown Court in Surrey, as to how he recognised a crook he saw climbing out of a window after burgling a house.

'I notice,' said the defence lawyer to the policeman, 'that you are wearing glasses.'

'Yes, sir,' he replied, 'they are my reading glasses.'

'Your eyesight is clearly defective,' continued the lawyer, 'and yet you ask us to believe that you recognised my client at a distance of fifty metres on a dark night.'

'Yes sir, there is nothing wrong with my distance sight. I only need glasses when I am reading.'

'When you say distance,' pushed the lawyer, 'just how far do you think you can see at night?'

'Well,' replied the policeman, rather losing his patience, 'on a clear night I can see the moon,'

A few weeks before, the same court had seen another lawyer try to catch a policeman out. Sergent Jones read his account of how, on a dark night, he had crept up on the man accused of the crime and had got close enough to recognise him. When it was the turn of the defence lawyer to ask questions. he strolled over to Sergeant Jones.

'I must say,' said the lawyer, 'that you are looking very smart today, Sergeant.'

'Thank you, sir,' said Jones not expecting such a compliment. 'I like to look presentable for the Force.'

'And do you always look so smart?'

'Oh yes, sir,' said Jones. 'I'm an old army man. Appearance is important when you're on duty.'

'And your boots,' said the lawyer, pointing at the gleaming hobnailed boots Jones was wearing, 'do you wear them for work?'

'Yes, sir. They are very comfortable for walking the beat.'

The lawyer nodded. 'I see' he said, 'I think we all noticed that your boots were very noisy as you walked up to the stand, with the nails crunching on the floor. How did you manage to creep up close to my client if you were wearing those?'

Jones didn't bat an eyelid. 'I rode my bike,' he replied.

Judge Rann, of New York, had a bizarre method of sentencing. Having just dealt with a shoplifting case, he looked up to see a very dirty and untidy man step into the dock.

'What is the charge?' he asked.

The Clerk stood up. 'This man, Jack String, is charged with unhygienic conditions in the food preparation area of his bakery.'

The judge glanced at the man again; he felt that anybody looking as dirty as String was bound to keep a dirty shop. Still, he thought, he had better listen to the evidence before making his mind up.

First into the witness box was the local health inspector.

'I conducted an inspection of String's Bakery on November 25th,' he said, 'and found the kitchen to be very dirty. I ordered Mr String to clean the room. On my return two weeks later the kitchen was still dirty, so I charged him with health crimes.'

Next into the stand was a senior health inspector who had been on the second visit.

'On the second visit to Mr String's bakery,' he said, 'I carried out a thorough investigation. I found dirt on the floor, in the oven and on the worktop where dough is mixed.'

Rann did not have much sympathy for the baker who, as he watched, scratched his arm, revealing a large stain on his jacket. Rann sighed.

'OK, Mr String,' he said. 'What would you like to say in your defence?'

'Gee, your honour,' he replied. 'These guys are so fussy. My place is clean enough. They were looking for things to find wrong!'

'I see,' said Rann. 'And tell me do you think that you are clean at the moment?'

String looked down at his scruffy shirt and rubbed his dirty, unshaven chin.

'Well,' he muttered. 'I reckon so. It's about as clean as I get.'

The judge took a deep breath. Obviously the man had no idea about hygiene. Giving him a stiff fine would punish him, but would probably have no effect on his bakery. Then he had an idea.

'It is the sentence of this court,' he said, in his most severe tone, 'that Jack String be taken from this court to the washroom upstairs and given a good scrubbing, especially behind the ears. Perhaps that will teach him what clean means. The court will now proceed to the washroom to see punishment carried out.'

Everybody then went upstairs to watch a policeman carry out the sentence.

A North Carolina judge called Hawkins also believed in making the punishment fit the crime. On one occasion he was in court dealing with a group of men who had all been found guilty of gambling with dice. Not only was gambling illegal in that state, but

Hawkins strongly disliked gambling himself. He wanted to teach the men a lesson they would not forget.

'Show me the dice they used,' said Hawkins.

The Clerk of the Court handed the two dice over. The judge rattled them around in his hand. As he did so he had an idea. A smile spread across his face.

'Come here, Wilkins,' he instructed one of the guilty men, who walked hesitantly across the courtroom to stand in front of him.

'Here,' he said 'take the dice. Since you like gambling so much, you can gamble with your future. Throw the dice and the number you throw will be how many months you get in jail.'

'Are you serious?' asked Wilkins.

'Very,' he snapped. 'Throw.'

Wilkins rolled the dice, scoring five.

'I hereby sentence this man to five months in jail.' declared the judge. He pointed across to another of the gamblers, who rolled a three.

The third man stared at the dice in his hand and began to sweat; then he rolled the dice on the counter. He scored a double six.

'Well done,' said Hawkins. 'You've just won yourself twelve months in jail. Perhaps that will teach you not to gamble. Next case please.'

A magistrate who tried a man for stealing a pair of boots from a shop was very impatient. The shop had lost several pairs during the previous week, so a plain-clothes policeman was on duty to keep an eye on customers who might be shoplifting. He had seen a man walk in, take off his old boots and put on a new pair, then walk out carrying his old ones. Naturally none of the staff bothered to stop a man carrying such a battered old pair of boots. Only the policeman, who had seen the switch, realised what had happened. He arrested the man.

When the case came to court, it was before a magistrate well-known for having no patience and particularly disliking policemen who did not give their evidence very clearly. Unfortunately, the policeman in this case became rather muddled.

The magistrate began to tap the desk, which made him even more nervous and flustered.

'Really,' muttered the magistrate, 'you must try to get your facts right.'

After a few more seconds he lost his patience completely.

'This is no good,' he complained, 'just tell us straight. Did the accused take his old boots off before or after putting on the new ones?'

It took the Clerk of the Court several minutes to control the laughter from the public gallery, but the magistrate spent rather longer trying to live down his mistake.

In a remote country town in New South Wales in 1903, a confidence trickster named Robert Butler was in court. He was known far and wide as 'Charming Charlie' because of the way he could talk money out of almost anybody, and he was charged with swindling people at a local horserace. The evidence was overwhelming and he was found guilty.

The magistrate eyed him coldly.

'You are guilty of a serious crime,' he said. 'And I have no alternative but to sentence you to six months in goal.'

The accused man looked glum at the stiff sentence.

'However,' continued the magistrate. 'I understand that you are an accomplished musician.'

'That's right,' said Charlie. 'I play the organ and the piano.'

'As I thought,' said the magistrate, 'Well, our local church is temporarily without an organist. I shall knock one day off your sentence for every wedding, funeral or service at which you agree to play the organ.'

Charlie grinned. 'I agree, your honour,' he said.

For the next few weeks he played his heart out on the church organ. He attended every service that was held and produced music far superior to anything the locals had ever heard. They were almost disappointed when, after four months, Charlie had worked off his sentence and left town.

In the American west during the 1880s the legal process was also rather rough and ready. Because of the vast distances between settlements and the lack of any regular communication, law courts were haphazard affairs. Minor offences were usually dealt with by local sheriffs and educated men who were willing to act as judges. There were, however, some genuine judges who travelled around, calling at towns from time to time to try cases. In the autumn of 1881 one such Judge, named Behan, arrived at a town without any warning.

He called on Sheriff Breckenridge and asked which cases were awaiting trial. The sheriff handed over documents relating to a number of cases for him to study. Next morning, court was convened and Judge Behan arrived.

'Now then,' he said to Breckenridge. 'It appears to me that the case of Johnny Ringo is the most urgent. The other matters are minor crimes, but Ringo is accused of robbing stage coaches and of shooting a barman dead.'

'Wouldn't you rather try someone else first and leave Ringo till last?' gasped Breckenridge.

Judge Behan looked at him. 'No, I would not. Bring Ringo here at once.'

'Er . . .' Breckenridge shuffled his feet. 'I can't.'

'Can't?' roared the judge 'Why not?'

He looked embarassed. 'Well,' he said. 'The truth is that I let him go.'

'Let him go?' Behan was astounded. 'This man is accused of robberty and murder and you let him go?'

'Yes. See we haven't got a real jail here and if Ringo wanted he could have broken out of it anyway. I made him promise not to rob anybody and to come back once a week to report to me.'

Behan was almost speechless. He could not believe what he was hearing.

'You mean you trust this Ringo?' he asked quietly.

'Oh yes,' said Breckenridge. 'He's a thief, a robber and a crook, but he has never lied. He'll be back on Thursday.'

Behan was surprised by the events in court, but even more surprised when Ringo did turn up to stand trial on Thursday.

Two years later, Judge Behan was once again shocked by what he heard in a Western court. He was hearing an inquiry into the death of a man named Baker who had been found lying in the street with a bullet in his chest. From the evidence of the witnesses it seemed that the man had been shot by a local gambler.

However, it soon became clear to Behan that the whole story was not coming out. For some reason the witnesses were not telling all they knew. He guessed that something had happened before the shooting which the townsfolk did not want to reveal to an outsider.

When the time came for a verdict, he turned to the jury and asked if they had reached a decision.

'We have, your honour,' said the foreman of the jury.

'What is your verdict?' he asked, expecting to hear him answer either murder or manslaughter.

'We find,' said the foreman, 'that Baker died because he was stupid enough to jump in front of a bullet.'

And so the matter rested.

A suspicious alibi was used by a burglar who came up for trial before Lord Justice Darling, who knew the crook well and had strong suspicions that he was guilty, and therefore called the defence lawyer to see him just as the trial began.

'I understand,' he said, 'that your defence is the alibi that your client was in Brighton on the night of the crime.'

'That is correct,' said the lawyer.

'Well,' said Darling, 'I think it only fair to warn you that if your client is found not guilty, I shall prosecute all his witnesses for perjury.'

Hearing this, the defence witnesses stood up and left at once. Clearly they did not want to risk lying if they were going to be hauled up in court themselves.

Fakes and Forgeries

'Fake!' gasped the prosecution lawyer. 'What do you mean, fake?'

Hans van Meergeren, the small, neatly dressed man in the dock, smiled. 'It is a fake,' he said. 'A worthless forgery.'

A stunned silence settled over the courtroom.

'Are you trying to tell me,' said the lawyer in hushed tones, 'that this painting, a picture recognised throughout the world as one of the great art treasures of the seventeenth century, is a fake? And you can prove it?'

'Yes,' replied van Meergeren. 'I painted it myself.'

The short exchange was the turning point in a famous trial held in Holland just after the Second World War. It was a trial which rocked Holland and the entire art world. Before it was over, the reputations of dozens of experts had been ruined and great museums had become laughing stocks. Nobody laughed harder then van Meergeren himself.

The long story which led to that trial began many years earlier when he left art college as an ambitious young artist. He was convinced that he could paint great pictures and wanted to be recognised by the art world. He produced a few small paintings, which were bought, but when he painted what he thought was his masterpiece, it was laughed at and went unsold. He felt deeply insulted and vowed revenge.

He happened to come across a book which told him that Michelangelo, one of the greatest sculptors of all time, first became famous as a forger. He used to carve copies of ancient Greek statues and pretend that he had dug them up in southern Italy. Van Meergeren decided that he would do the same thing. He wanted not only to earn money but also to trick the art experts who had sneered at his work.

He knew he would have to be very careful. The experts were no fools and would spot a clumsy fake straight away. First he studied the works of the old Dutch masters. He found that a seventeenth century painter, Vermeer, had produced many pictures which had since been lost. Perfect, he thought; he could fake the lost pictures and then pretend to have found them somewhere.

Next he went to work on the materials. He found out how paints were made in the seventeenth century, studied Vermeer's style and how he had applied paint to the canvas and, finally, practised making new paintings look old by baking them in an oven, painting them with dirt and rolling them up to produce age cracks. All this was done in his spare time. It took four years, but at long last he was ready to begin.

He bought a cheap seventeenth century painting and stripped most of the paint off it. leaving a genuinely old canvas. Then he painted a depiction of *Christ and his Disciples at Emmaeus* in the style of Vermeer. He added Vermeer's initials and then put the finished painting through his special ageing process. Then he went to see a famous art dealer named Helmond.

'I have come to see you on a very delicate matter.' said van Meergeren. 'I assume I can trust you to absolute secrecy.'

'Of course.' replied Helmond.

'I am the friend of an aristocratic family who own several magnificent paintings. Unfortunately the family is short of money. They do not wish to admit this in public so they have decided to sell one of their paintings privately. I cannot tell you their name, of course, but I assure you that they are honourable people who will be satisfied with a fair price.'

Helmond was used to dealing with impoverished nobles and knew how to respect their pride.

'I understand completely,' said Helmond. 'What is this painting?'

'It is a work by Vermeer called *Christ and his Disciples at Emmaeus.*'

Helmond raised his eyebrows. 'Such a work would be worth a great deal of money.'

'I hope so.' replied van Meergeren. 'My friends are in need of it.'

The next day he called on the dealer again, bringing with him his fake painting. Helmond inspected it and was convinced that it was genuine. He arranged to sell it to a French businessman who loved old Dutch paintings. He received over £100,000 for it then pocketed his commission and gave the rest to van Meergeren, who was overjoyed. He had hoodwinked the experts and made a small fortune. Back at his studio he quickly produced a second fake Vermeer and sold that for an even higher price.

Soon afterwards the Frenchman who had bought the first fake died and his son put it up for public auction. It created a sensation. This was the first time that the world as a whole got to hear about the 'rediscovered' painting. A great expert inspected the painting before its sale. He studied it long and hard, putting it through various scientific tests, and finally pronounced it genuine. It was bought by Amsterdam's Boymans Museum for even more than van Meergeren had been paid.

At first he was worried by this turn of events. He feared that with the painting being studied by so many experts, one of them might spot that it was a fake. He need not have been concerned. Everyone was taken in by the forgery and it was put on display at the museum. The picture was hailed as the greatest art find of the century.

When van Meergeren appeared with yet another 'rediscovery' he found that prices had spiralled and that his new painting was worth several times more than the first. He was delighted.

At this point fate took a hand. The Second World War broke out and Holland was invaded by the Germans. Van Meergeren began producing fakes especially to sell to the Germans. One of these, *Christ and the Adulteress*, was recognised as perhaps the most important painting from the seventeenth century. He produced several more fake Vermeers and other works which he sold for colossal amounts of money. The profits were carefully stored in a secret Swiss bank account. Though highly profitable, the sales to Germans caused van Meergeren's downfall.

After the defeat of Germany, the Dutch authorities prosecuted anyone who had helped the Germans more than they had to. They believed that van Meergeren had been selling off Holland's aritistic heritage and charged him with collaboration.

At his trial the prosecution gathered a mass of evidence proving that he had sold paintings to the Germans, including the magnificent *Christ and the Adulteress*. As the court case proceeded, van Meergeren realised that there was only one way he could avoid a long prison sentence for collaborating.

When called upon to offer evidence in his defence, he calmly announced that he had not collaborated and had been swindling the Germans, not helping them. The paintings, he said, were fakes. This announcement startled everyone.

At first nobody believed him; they thought he was lying in order to avoid going to prison. Several art experts were called to court to give evidence that the paintings were genuine. With more evidence piling up against him, van Meergeren decided on a dramatic gesture.

'I can prove I produced the fakes,' he said. 'Let me work in my studio for a few weeks and I'll produce another perfect forgery.'

The judge agreed that this was the only way to prove the truth of the artist's claims so he was given a police escort and sent back to his studio. Experts were allowed in to see him work. Beneath the eyes of the men who had accepted the fakes as genuine, van Meergeren produced a painting called *The Young Christ*. It was as perfect as his earlier pictures.

The charges of collaboration were dropped, but he was instantly arrested for forgery. He was found guilty and sent to prison for a few months. On his release, he bought a house in France and retired. Every few months he went to Switzerland to draw money out of his secret account. He died ten years after his sensational trial.

A Hungarian painter called Elmyr de Hory was an even more daring forger. Not content with forging old masters, he faked modern paintings by artists who were still alive. However, he never put a false signature on his work. He hoped that if he were ever arrested he could plead that he was selling his own paintings not fakes. He would pose as a collector in sudden need of cash who wanted to sell a few pictures, and contacted various galleries throughout the world, selling a few pictures to each.

One day he happened to be at a gallery, trying to sell some paintings, when the great Spanish artist Pablo Picasso paid a visit. One of the pictures de Hory was selling was a fake Picasso. Seeing the artist, he had an amazing idea.

He strolled over with the fake tucked under his arm.

'Excuse me, Señor Picasso,' he said. 'I don't know if you remember me, but I bought this painting from you a couple of years ago. Unfortunately you did not sign it. I was wondering if you would do so now?'

Picasso glanced down at it.

'Of course,' he said, and signed.

De Hory then promptly sold the picture for a small fortune.

It was de Hory who provided the inspiration for a hoax on a truly colossal scale, although he had no way of knowing what he had started. In 1966 an American writer named Clifford Irving wrote a book called *Fake* about de Hory and his amazing adventures. While preparing the research it occured to Irving that he could pull off a similar hoax himself. But Irving was not an artist, he was a writer. Since he could not fake paintings, he decided to fake a book.

In part, he was spurred on by the same disappointment which had affected van Meergeren. He had written several books, but they had not sold well and were not praised by critics. He wanted to write a bestseller.

He began looking around for a suitable subject and in 1968 he found it. He learnt that the multi-millionaire and international businessman Howard Hughes had not been seen in public since 1957. He would make the perfect subject for the hoax.

Hughes lived as a total recluse, seeing only a handful of close friends. His business deals were arranged by telephone so that even the people who worked for him had not seen him. Earlier in life, however, he had been a very public figure. He had run a movie studio and had sponsored the largest aircraft ever built up to that time. He had been friends with politicians and movie stars. Then suddenly he had abandoned everything and become a hermit. Nobody was even certain where he lived.

Irving thought this provided the perfect opportunity for his fraud. He knew that many books had been written about Hughes and that they had sold well, earning vast amounts of money. However, he noticed that none of them was accepted as a genuine account of his life. Irving decided to fake an autobiography. Such a book, he knew, would make a fortune.

Soon after having the idea, he wrote to his publishers, McGraw-Hill, He said, 'I sent a copy of *Fake* some time ago to Howard Hughes, and to my surprise received a note of thanks and praise from him.' Irving went on to say that he had written to Hughes several times since and had received several letters in return. He then asked if a good biography had ever been produced although he knew no such book existed.

McGraw-Hill responded by asking Irving to visit them.

'You can see in this letter,' he said, handing a sheet of paper to the editor, 'that Hughes wants to produce an autobiography. He wants to put right all the mistakes made in other books about him.'

The editor took the letter; it was signed 'Howard R. Hughes' and stated that he was annoyed by all the lies which had been told about him. The editor was very excited, as Irving had known he would be.

'You mean Hughes is actually willing to write his life story for us?' the man gasped.

'Willing to?' asked Irving, 'He wants to!'

'Wait here,' instructed the editor. He left the room and returned soon afterwards with the directors of the company.

They read through the letters signed 'Howard R. Hughes' and were also impressed. They agreed to pay the massive sum of half a million dollars for the book. This would be paid in three parts; $100,000 straight away, the same sum when research was finished and the remainder when the manuscript was completed and delivered to them. The cheques were to be given to Irving who would pass them on to Howard Hughes.

When the contract was drawn up, the publishers wanted Hughes to come and sign it. Irving explained that he never left his secret home. However, he offered to take the contract away and get it signed. The publishers agreed.

He left with the contract and carefully forged Hughes's signature, then brought it back.

Over the following few weeks McGraw-Hill received several letters signed 'Howard Hughes'. He asked the publishers to keep the project completely secret. They assumed that this was simply part of his well-known liking for secrecy.

Irving knew that he was cheating the publishers. More to the point as soon as news of the book leaked out, Hughes himself would hear about it. He was not certain what he would do. Hughes might step forward and denounce the book or, alternatively, he might stay silent for fear of attracting publicity.

Whatever happened, Irving believed he would make a fortune. If Hughes spoke out, he would already have the $500,000 in his pocket and could flee abroad. If he stayed silent, Irving would continue to make money as more and more copies were sold.

Over the following months, Irving went to work. He read everything he could find about Howard Hughes. He bought other people's books and read old issues of newspapers. He also watched dozens of old newsreels showing Hughes in his younger days. From these sources he gathered enough material to write a biography. He even picked up special words and phrases Hughes liked to use.

Irving began writing and produced a book which was actually quite a good biography. If he had written it under his own name, he might have had the book published anyway, but stood to earn far more money by faking an autobiography.

In 1971, the manuscript was complete. He handed it over and sat back to wait.

The publishers read it through and were impressed. They noticed the little phrases which Irving had worked in and checked the facts mentioned in the book. They tallied with the truth. Thinking they had a bestseller on their hands, they paid the remainder of the money.

The cheques were made out to 'H.R. Hughes', but that didn't worry Irving. He got his wife to open a bank account in the name of Helga R. Hughes.

Meanwhile McGraw-Hill had been trying to authenticate the book. They asked handwriting experts to look at the letters and the signature on the contract. They confirmed that the writing was that of Howard Hughes and didn't spot the forgery. A date was set for publication of the book and an announcement made in the world's newspapers.

It was at this point that disaster struck for Irving. A journalist received a telephone call from Howard Hughes, whom he had known some years earlier. Hughes said he had never met Irving and that the book was a total forgery.

The journalist told McGraw-Hill about the phone call and they contacted Irving, who tried to wriggle out of the problem by claiming that the man who phoned the journalist was an imposter. But a few weeks later Hughes issued an official announcement stating that he knew nothing about the book.

The police charged Irving with fraud and deception, and at the trial he was found guilty and sentenced to three years in jail.

Possibly the most audacious art fakers in history

were the South Americans Yves Chaudron and
Eduardo de Valfierno. Early in their careers the two
perfected a scheme for gaining money which never
failed them. But eventually they aimed too high and
were caught.

The original scheme was simple but effective. First
they would contact any art dealer or collector who
was not too fussy about where pictures came from,
and there were plenty of those in South America.
Then they would explain that they could steal any
picture to order. The crooked dealer would name a
painting he wanted stolen and Chaudron and Valfierno then went to work faking the required painting.
When the fake was complete they would stage a
phoney break-in at the gallery or home where the
genuine painting was kept. This would, of course, be
reported in the newspapers, whereupon the pair
would turn up with the fake claiming it was the original. The dealer would gleefully pay them and they
would then take the money and run. When the dealer
found out he had been duped he could hardly go to
the police; if he did he would be accused of attempted
robbery, which made it a perfect scheme with little
risk involved.

Unfortunately they had soon played their trick on
most of the dishonest dealers in South America. They
decided to move their operations to Europe. For some
months they did well, producing and selling numerous
fakes. But one fateful day in 1911, Chaudron read an
article in a Paris newspaper. His eyes scanned the
page quickly then he turned to Valfierno.

'It says here that the Mona Lisa is the biggest
attraction in the Louvre Museum,' he declared.

'So?'

'So, how much do you think the mugs would pay if they thought we'd stolen it?'

Valfierno stared at his friend. 'You're not thinking of pulling our trick with the Mona Lisa, are you?'

'Why not?' demanded Chaudron.

'I'll tell you why not! Because the Mona Lisa is so famous and so valuable that any newspaper report of a raid on the Louvre is bound to say that the Mona Lisa is untouched. Nobody would ever believe we'd stolen it.'

Chaudron thought for a moment. 'But what if we really did steal it?'

'Are you crazy? We're forgers not burglars! We couldn't steal it if we tried. Anyway, the money we got for it wouldn't be worth the risk.'

Chaudron grinned wickedly. 'Listen,' he said. 'We could really clean up here. And then retire to a life of luxury.'

Valfierno eyed his friend sceptically. 'How?'

'Look, suppose we fake the painting before stealing it. Then we'd be able to sell both the fake and the real painting. The mugs buying it would keep quiet about having what they think is the real thing. We could sell as many fakes as we wanted.'

Valfierno frowned. 'But how would we get the real painting to start with? Like I said we aren't burglars.'

'No,' said Chaudron, 'but what about our old friend Perugia? We could hire him to do the job.'

That night they explained their plan to Perugia.

'The Mona Lisa is heavily guarded,' he replied thoughtfully. 'It won't be an easy job.'

Chaudron and Valfierno looked disappointed. 'Does that mean you can't do it?' they asked.

'I don't know,' he said 'I'll need to spend several days at the museum to see how they organise their guards.'

He left for the Louvre next day. Three weeks later he reappeared, excited and breathless.

'I can do it!' he gasped. 'I know how to do it!'

'How?' asked Chaudron impatiently.

'Aha,' said Perugia tapping his nose. 'That's my secret. If I tell you that you won't need me any more. But I'll tell you this; you can start on your fakes. Just tell me when you want the picture pinched.'

The very next day Valfierno set to work faking the Mona Lisa. He discovered how the artist, Leonardo da Vinci, had made his paints and what type of canvas he had used. He quickly recreated these and then began spending long hours at the museum studying the picture. Finally he was ready and began to work on a canvas.

Meanwhile Chaudron had been busy travelling. He had visited many dealers and collectors in Europe and America. Paying special attention to those with shady reputations, he hinted that he had a major work of art to sell. He was always careful to check if a prospective client was really crooked before revealing which painting was up for offer. He did not want an honest man giving the game away.

Eventually, he lined up six crooks willing to part with $300,000 each for what they thought was to be the real Mona Lisa. Valfierno produced six fakes to fit the order. Then they went to Perugia.

'Everything's ready,' they said. 'We want the picture stolen.'

'Fine,' he replied, 'but I shall need your help.'

'What do we have to do?'

'First we wait until next week, when the Louvre is going to be closed for cleaning, then we get to work.'

The following Thursday, the day before the museum was closed, he called on his friends, carrying a large bag in his hand. He led them to the museum which they entered as ordinary tourists. Once inside, however, Perugia ignored the galleries and led the forgers down into the basement where they hid in a dirty storeroom.

'Now what?' they asked.

Perugia grinned. 'Now we wait,' he said, taking out some bread and cheese from his bag and passing them round.

They stayed in the cellar all night. When the sounds of movement next morning told them that there were people in the museum, Perugia opened his bag again and pulled out some clothes.

'Here we go.' he said. 'Put these on. They're the uniforms of the firm doing the cleaning. I stole them a few weeks back.'

The three crooks changed into the uniforms then climbed the stairs to the galleries. Grabbing brooms and brushes, they mingled with the workers until they reached the gallery where the Mona Lisa was kept. They casually lifted the picture from the wall and pretended to be dusting it.

Then they simply walked off with it. Nobody stopped them or asked them what they were doing.

Everyone assumed that they were part of the cleaning team and were acting on orders.

When the museum staff found the picture was missing, there was uproar. The police were informed and the papers published the news of the most daring crime of the decade.

Chaudron and Valfierno loved it. Their clients would see the newspapers and know the picture was stolen. They parcelled up the fakes and sent them off, receiving the promised cash in return.

Then disaster struck. Perugia betrayed his colleagues, stole the genuine Mona Lisa from its hiding place and fled to Italy. There he attempted to sell it but was spotted by the police and caught. He informed on the others and soon all three found themselves in jail.

Imposters and Phoneys

Arthur Orton very nearly became the most successful and richest imposter of all time. Instead he spent ten years in prison and died in poverty. His impersonation grabbed headlines around the world and yet it began quite modestly in the town of Wagga Wagga, in Australia.

He was the town butcher, but was not a very good businessman. To add to his troubles he loved gambling and was soon deeply in debt. On a fateful Wednesday morning, his landlord came to see him about unpaid rent. He saw the landlord approaching and knew he had to think fast.

'Good morning, Mr Ticknor,' he said, smiling broadly.

'Is it?' asked Ticknor grumpily. 'We'll see about that. I've come about the rent. You owe me nearly thirty pounds.'

He was worried, but did not want to show it and smiled even more broadly.

'Oh yes,' he said. 'I'm sorry I've taken so long over paying you, but I'm waiting for my family in England to send me some money.' He was lying, he had no family in England, but he hoped to put off paying for a few more weeks.

'Family?' asked Ticknor in surprise. 'I thought that you were an orphan.'

'Oh no,' said Orton, looking round to make sure nobody was listening. 'I just put that story around to fool people. My family is really very wealthy, but I ran away from them some years ago to seek my fortune in Australia.'

Ticknor eyed Orton suspiciously. He didn't trust the man, but if his story was true, it would be worth waiting.

'I'll tell you what,' continued Orton, 'If you give me a month until my money comes through I'll pay you forty pounds instead of thirty.'

That seemed a good bargain to Ticknor, so he agreed.

The month passed, and Orton still had no money. He had, however, been doing some research. He read in local newspapers that an English noble family named Tichborne were trying to find the heir to their estate, who had vanished in a shipwreck in 1854 – eleven years earlier. The paper went on to say that the Tichbornes were very rich.

Orton had an idea.

When his landlord and other people to whom he owed money came to visit him, he had a new story prepared. First he showed them the newspaper story about the Tichborne family.

'There you are,' he said. 'I'm the missing heir, Roger Tichborne. As soon as I get the money from my family, and you can see from the newspaper report that they are very rich, I shall pay you everything I owe you.'

The tradesmen of Wagga Wagga were impressed. They believed that he was the missing heir. After all, they reasoned, he was a bit eccentric and he might well have been a rich man on the run from his responsibilities, so they settled back to await their money.

Unfortunately for Orton, a newspaper reporter got to hear about the supposed British aristocrat living in Wagga Wagga as a butcher. He published an enthusiastic story about 'Roger Tichborne' and how he enjoyed living in Australia far more than enjoying his wealth in England.

He was horrified. He had never intended that so many people should know about his lies. He had only wanted to delay paying his bills. He hurriedly called all his creditors together to make an announcement.

'I'm terribly sorry to have to tell you this,' he said, 'but I have some bad news. I wrote to my family in England, the Tichbornes, but they have refused to send me any money. They have said that they do not believe I am Roger Tichborne.'

There was a long silence.

'Now,' he continued. 'If you will all give me a few days to collect some money I shall be able to start paying my debts.'

He waited to see what would happen. Would the people order his arrest for debt or would they agree to be paid in instalments?

'That's terrible,' said one man.

'Awful,' said another.

'We'll help you,' said a third.

'Help me?' asked Orton. 'How do you mean?'

'You must go to England and claim your inheritance,' said Ticknor. 'We'll pay for you to go, so long as you promise to pay us back when you get your money.'

He was shocked. His lies had forced him into a difficult position. Either he could admit that he had lied, and risk being thrown into gaol, or he could go to London. Faced with such a choice, Orton decided on the second option.

He arrived in England to find it agog with interest. Newspapermen met him off his ship and wanted to interview him. Everywhere he went, he was a celebrity. Perhaps for the first time, he realised what he had done.

In order to avoid being charged with fraud, he had to push his claim. He thought he ought to find something out about Roger Tichborne and must have been very worried by what he discovered. Roger had been slim, athletic and a great scholar. Orton was fat, lazy and could barely read.

Nevertheless when he was introduced to Lady Tichborne, Roger's mother, he managed to convince her that he was her son. Perhaps the elderly lady wanted so much to believe that her son was alive that she would have accepted anyone who approached her.

Roger's brother, Alfred, was not so certain. He believed the man to be a fraud. A few months after he arrived, Alfred died and his son Henry took over the vast Tichborne inheritance. The family was split over whether Henry should have the estate or whether Orton should, assuming that he was Roger.

Hoping to get to the bottom of the mystery, Henry, who had not known Roger very well, decided to set a test. He invited several of Roger's friends to devise a series of questions to which Roger, but nobody else, would know the answers. The questions dealt with details of his childhood, his favourite toys, events at school and other trivial details which Orton would be unable to find in newspapers.

He failed hopelessly, getting most of the questions utterly wrong. This did not stop him starting a civil action against Henry, alleging that he had illegally taken the Tichborne inheritance while Roger was still alive.

He borrowed huge amounts of money to pay for his legal bills on the strength of his claim to be Roger. The case began on 11 May 1871 and dragged on for months, becoming a highly controversial issue. All of Britain and much of Europe took sides. Even music hall comedians began making fun of the Tichborne family.

Finally, in March 1872 the court decided that Henry had not acted illegally in taking the inheritance. The police immediately arrested Orton on charges of impersonation for gain. The new trial lasted nearly two years. At the end of it all, Orton's true identity was discovered and he was sentenced to fourteen years in jail. He was released after ten years, confessed to his crimes and lived the rest of his life in poverty.

Also successful, for a short period of time, was Wilhelm Voigt, who pulled off one of the most astounding impersonations of modern history. His crime was performed one afternoon in October 1906 and was the result of something he had seen a few weeks earlier.

He had been standing in a street in his native Berlin when a party of soldiers came marching past. This was not unusual, for many soldiers were stationed in Berlin. As the men marched past, however, an army officer stopped them and gave them some orders. He noticed that the officer wore the uniform of a different regiment, yet the soldiers obeyed him.

He had an idea.

He went to see a tailor and told him that he wanted a fancy dress outfit. He handed over photos of the uniforms worn by an army captain. He was careful to use the uniforms of a regiment stationed a few miles outside Berlin. He hoped it would be familiar to Berlin troops, but that he would not actually run into any member of that regiment.

As soon as the uniform was finished, he went into action. He put on the uniform and marched out into the street, moving and behaving with the pride and decisiveness he had seen in real officers. After a few minutes he found half a dozen soldiers moving through the streets. He marched up to them.

'Corporal,' he snapped.

'Yes, sir,' replied the corporal jumping to attention and saluting smartly.

'I have a job for you and your men,' he aid. 'Follow me.'

He turned on his heel and marched across the street hearing the boots of the soldiers following him. He smiled. They had been convinced.

He led them to the town hall of Kopenick, a suburb of Berlin, and marched straight past the doorman, then stopped an official.

'You,' he boomed. 'Where are the offices of Mayor Schmidt?'

The man looked at him and at his men, assuming that they had decided to visit the mayor.

'At the end of the corridor, sir,' he told Voigt. 'the last door on the right.'

Voigt turned to his men. 'Come on,' he ordered. 'And keep your guns ready. He might get difficult.'

The soldiers wondered what was happening, but they did not dare question him. Ever since joining the German army they had been trained to follow orders instantly and without question. They knew that severe punishments were handed out to those who disobeyed orders.

Voigt barged straight into the mayor's office, followed by his men.

'Are you Mayor Schmidt?' he asked curtly.

A small man with a moustache looked up from behind a desk.

'Yes.' He looked alarmed.

'Right,' said Voigt. 'General Hikmann has reason to believe that you or your deputy are stealing money from the wages box.'

'You must be mistaken!' protested the mayor.

'The army is not mistaken,' he snapped. 'Fetch the wages box at once.'

The Mayor, overawed by his commanding tone of voice, called his secretary and asked her to bring the box of money.

'Open it,' ordered Voigt.

The mayor unlocked the case and lifted the lid to reveal a mound of gold and silver coins. Voigt eyed it without apparent interest.

'How much money is supposed to be here?' he asked.

The mayor consulted his cash book.

'These are the weekly wages of all staff who work

in the town hall itself,' he said. 'There are five thousand two hundred and fifty marks in the box.'

'Are there? We shall soon see about that,' snapped Voigt, and turned to his men.

'Corporal, keep this man and his secretary here under close arrest until I return. I am going to count this money.'

With that, he picked up the box and left the room, marched along the corridor and out of the town hall. Racing home, he burned his uniform and hid the cash.

Back at the town hall, the corporal began to grow uneasy. The strange officer was taking a long time to count the money. Eventually it dawned on him that he was not coming back. He telephoned General Hikmann.

'Excuse me, sir, but did you send a captain to question the Mayor about his cash box?'

'No,' snapped the General, 'of course not. Why should I?'

The next telephone call the corporal made was to the police. For some days they scoured Berlin looking for the 'Captain of Kopenick'. It was some weeks before Voigt was recognised and arrested. Meanwhile the whole German public had enjoyed a good laugh at the expense of the army officers who liked to be obeyed.

Another extraordinary impersonation was that of the 'Princes of Abyssinia' who visited Weymouth in 1910. They were not princes at all but the friends of a rich aristocrat called William de Vere Cole, who had a rather twisted sense of humour.

He had decided that it would be an extremely funny joke to make fools out of senior officers of the Royal

Navy. He was joined by some friends, including the famous author Virginia Woolf. The plans for the trick were laid well.

First Cole hired a make-up artist named Clarkson to change the appearance of his friends, then he found out the name of the admiral commanding the Atlantic Fleet, anchored at Weymouth. On the morning of the hoax, Cole swung into action.

He sent a telegram to the Admiral telling him that a secret visit of Abyssinian princes was taking place. He asked the officer to arrange an inspection tour of HMS *Dreadnought*, the largest battleship in the fleet. He signed the telegram Sir Charles Hardinge, the name of a senior official at the Foreign Office.

When the officers received the telegram they began preparing at once, making the ship and its crew as smart as possible.

Then they hurried down to Weymouth Railway Station to greet their visitors.

Cole, meanwhile, had dressed himself in his smartest clothes, complete with top hat. He marched to Paddington Railway Station and stopped a porter.

'Where can I find the stationmaster?' demanded Cole.

'He'll be up in his office, sir,' replied the porter, pointing towards a flight of steps.

'Thank you,' he said and hurried over to the steps. He found a door at the top and burst through without knocking.

'Are you the stationmaster?' he said to a man sitting at a desk.

'Yes, sir,' replied the startled man.

'Right,' said Cole. 'I am Herbert Cholmondely of

the Foreign Office. I need a special train to take a party of foreign princes to Weymouth.'

'When for?' asked the stationmaster.

'Now.'

'Now?' he gasped.

'Yes. Here's the money; now jump to it.' He laid a wad of notes on the table.

The stationmaster swept up the notes and rushed off to find a spare engine and some coaches. Within half an hour, everything was ready. Cole went to fetch his friends and ushered them on to the train as if they really were royalty.

When the train arrived in Weymouth, the imposters were met by a party of naval officers. Again Cole pretended to be Cholmondely and ushered the 'princes' forward. They pretended that they could not speak English. Instead they chatted to each other in Latin. Cole pretended to translate into English.

The unsuspecting naval officers led the party to a carriage which took them to the dockside. There they were ushered aboard HMS *Dreadnought*. For the following hour they enjoyed a guided tour of the ship. The officers were only too happy to show them around. They offered the visitors a magnificent spread of food and drink, but the so-called princes had to say no. They had been warned that their make-up would run if they ate or drank anything!

After a delightful visit, they left to return to London by another special train. The cost of the trick, including trains, make-up and costumes amounted to nearly £4,000 and Cole paid the lot happily, all for the sake of a good laugh.

Amazing Pranks

Faced by overwhelming evidence of guilt, many crooks have tried to establish an alibi by proving that they were elsewhere when the crime was committed. Usually such false alibis are revealed at trial, but a man named John Nevison once established an alibi which saved him from being hanged.

Nevison was a highwayman, famous for making fast escapes on the bay horse which he rode when robbing coaches. At four o'clock in the morning on 5 May 1668, Nevison held up a coach at Gads Hill, just south of London. Not until he was robbing the passengers did he recognise one of them as a man who had once been his next-door-neighbour.

He paused and readjusted his mask. So long as it was in place, he was safe.

'Come on,' he said waving a pistol at an old man on the coach. 'Hand over your money.'

The man dug deep into his pockets and pulled out a purse which he tossed to Nevison.

'And your watch.'

Reluctantly, the man took his watch from his pocket and gave him that, too. As he did so, it slipped out of his hand and, bending to pick it up, Nevison felt his mask slip. He made a desperate grab, but was too late; the mask fell to the ground.

He glanced up quickly. His ex-neighbour was staring at him in surprise. He knew he had been recognised. Turning his horse around, he galloped off at high speed. A mile or so from the scene of the crime, he stopped.

Gazing back across the heath behind him, he was glad to see that he was not being followed, but he knew that he was in trouble. The man had recognised him and would be able to identify him in court. He knew that he had to think quickly and try to establish that he had not robbed the coach on Gads Hill. The easiest way to do that would be to convince people that he was somewhere else at the time.

A slow smile spread across his face. He patted his horse's back.

'I hope you're feeling fit, old girl,' he said. 'I've got a lot to ask of you today.

With a swift kick he set off at a smart trot towards London. He would try to get as far as possible before nightfall and then establish his presence in whatever area he had reached.

Arriving in Tilbury, he took a ferry across the Thames and set out at a canter for the north. He reached Chelmsford at breakfast time and stopped for a rest. Striding into an inn, he ordered a meal for himself and a bag of feed for his horse. In less than an hour he was off again.

Knowing that his very life depended on how fast he rode, he urged his horse on at a gallop which brought her to a foaming sweat. By mid-morning, he was on the Great North Road and was travelling north as fast as he could. At Huntingdon, he stopped for a brief rest, then remounted and set off again.

As dusk began to fall, he rode into York, stabled

his horse, quickly brushed himself down and raced to the bowling green, where he knew the wealthy men of the city would be gathered. He spotted the Mayor of York and hurried over to him.

'Good evening, your worship,' he said.

'Good evening, sir,' replied the mayor.

'I was wondering if you could tell me the time?

The mayor glanced at his watch.

'It's a quarter to eight.' Nevison thanked him and strolled off.

When he came to trial for the robbery, he produced the Mayor of York as a witness to state that he was two hundred and thirty miles from the crime just fifteen hours later. The judge decided that no man could travel such a distance in such a short time and dismissed the charge.

A few years before Nevison's ride to York, Claude Duval was riding across Hampstead Heath. He was happy with life. He had come to England in 1661 as the penniless groom of an impoverished knight and now, just four years later, he was dressed in the finest fashions and had a pocket full of gold coins jingling at his side as he rode on a magnificent chestnut horse.

He had become a highwayman, robbing travellers on the lonely roads between towns and villages. But he was no ordinary robber. He always tried to avoid hurting his victims and was unfailingly polite to everybody.

As he rode along, chatting to his gang, Duval suddenly saw a coach in the distance.

'Hold lads,' he cried. 'It looks as if we might catch ourselves a victim today, after all.' He pointed towards the coach. 'That fine coach belongs to a rich man, no doubt.'

Ordering his gang to cover him with their pistols, he waited for his quarry to arrive. As it drew level, he stepped forward and signalled to the driver to halt. Realising he was faced by robbers, the man attempted to drive on, but Duval produced a pistol and threatened to fire. The coach came to a hurried stop.

'What's going on?' demanded a passenger's voice from inside. A man poked his head out of the coach window, to find himself staring down the barrel of Duval's pistol.

'I beg your pardon for stopping you like this,' he said. 'But I'm afraid that I'm rather short of money. I was wondering if you would be kind enough to give me some of yours'.

The man looked up. 'How dare you!' he gasped. 'You rogue!'

'Now, sir,' said Duval. 'There is no call for insults. You are a gentleman with money and I am a gentleman without money, so perhaps you would be kind enough to put this matter to rights.'

The man grunted and disappeared back into the coach, then he reappeared and held out a heavy purse. Duval bent forwards to take it, and then saw someone else was in the coach. He looked closer and saw that it was an extremely pretty young lady. He leaned back in his saddle. The time had come for one of his more enjoyable pranks.

Sliding from his horse, he quickly opened the coach door, smiled broadly and bowed low, sweeping off his hat as he did so.

'Your pardon, my lady,' he said. 'But it is a long

time since I had the pleasure of a dance with a lady as beautiful as yourself. I would deem it a great honour if you would give me a dance.'

'A dance?' she gasped.

Hesitantly, and rather nervously, she climbed down onto the green turf which bordered the road. Duval smiled and bowed again.

'Charles,' he said, turning to one of his men, 'did you bring your lute?' The man nodded, and reached for the instrument which was slung across his back. 'Then play us a dance tune,' said Duval. He began to strum the strings, picking out a lively tune with a catchy beat.

Taking the young woman by the hand, Duval slung her around. Rather bemused, she followed the steps which she knew so well from her dancing lessons. For some minutes the couple danced on the heath, as gracefully as if they were in a London ballroom.

When the music came to an end, Duval bowed to the lady and helped her back into the coach. Then he turned to the man still sitting there.

'I am sorry to have held you up for so long,' he said. 'Here is your money back. The pleasure of dancing with your charming daughter was worth many times that amount.'

Duval gazed into the startled eyes of the man, then leapt on to his horse and galloped off, laughing. He had lost the chance of making some money, but his reputation for gallantry was bound to be helped by his strange actions.

An unusual line of enquiry led to the conviction of a spy ring in 1989. The story began in 1986 when Clifford Stoll, an American astronomer, received the

telephone bill for his observatory in California. On it was a charge for 75c which did not match up with his own record of calls.

He soon found that the charge was due to someone ringing into his exchange and then connecting his call to the Cellnet computer. It was a charge for computer time which had come up. He decided to try and track down the crook who was using his computer link at the observatory's expense.

The strange calls continued and Stoll was alarmed to see that the unknown caller was linking into defence programmes and trying to extract informaton. He therefore devised a dummy package based on the Strategic Defence Initiative programme. When the unknown caller linked into the programme the call was automatically traced back to Hanover in Germany.

He alerted the FBI who stepped in at once. They located the caller and monitored his actions. It turned out that he and seven other Russian spies had been linking into various computers throughout Europe and America to extract information. And they were caught simply because Stoll became worried about an extra 75 cents on his bill.

A magician named Bendo had better luck; one day he was walking along Madison Avenue in New York; as he pushed his way through the crowded shopping street, he suddenly bumped into a man, who apologised.

'That's all right,' laughed Bendo. 'I should look where I'm going in future!'

Moments later, he entered a shop to buy a newspaper. When he reached for his wallet he found it had gone. Guessing that it had been stolen by the man he had bumped into, he dashed outside.

He could see the man a short distance away, and squirmed through the crowds to reach him. Using his skills as a conjurer, he took his wallet back from the thief's pocket without him realising, then returned to the shop to pay for the paper!

One of the most unusual tricks used by a thief was developed by Philip Welles who burgled several houses in London. The police were baffled by reports that burglar alarms in the area kept being set off for no apparent reason. Whenever the householder went to investigate the alarm he would find nobody present, nor any disturbance. One or two people found an open window, but no trace of an intruder.

It was not until the police caught Welles with a load of stolen property one night that the mystery was cleared up. Trotting at his heels was a small black terrier.

'Why did you bring your dog with you?' asked Constable Chadwick, during questioning at the police station.

'I like the company,' replied Welles.

Chadwick thought he was lying and believed that the dog helped him in his thefts. To test his theory, he took the dog outside to the rear of the police station. He arranged for a window to be left open. He would climb in and then ask a fellow police officer to approach the window. Perhaps the dog would bark a warning when somebody approached.

As it turned out, he did not have time to test this idea. As soon as he opened the rear window, the dog leapt up and scrambled through the opening. As he watched in amazement, it scampered around the room and then leapt out again, panting eagerly.

That was when Chadwick realised what had been happening. When Welles tried to burgle a home he first let the dog in through the window. By running round the room it would set off any alarms in the house. This gave him time to escape. When the house-holder came to investigate, he would be out of sight while the little black dog would be nearly invisible at night. If it did not set off an alarm Welles knew he could ransack the house with ease. It was a clever trick which worked for a while.

A man named Jim Moran used a very different trick in Los Angeles in 1949. In that year the Emir Saud, Crown Prince of Saudi Arabia, paid a visit to America. The fabulously wealthy prince was a great sensation, especially when he arrived in Hollywood to see the sights.

It was at this point that Moran decided to pull his trick. Hearing that the prince was going to spend a quiet evening at his hotel, without any official engage-ments, he phoned the extremely smart Ciro's restaurant.

'Good morning,' he said, 'this is Ibn Hajid, a ser-vant of his Royal Highness Emir Saud.'

'One moment,' said the amazed waiter, 'I shall pass you over to our manager.' There was a slight pause and then the manager came on the line.

'Hello,' he said. 'This is the manager speaking; how can we help you?'

'I would like to book a table for tonight for His Royal Highness,' said Moran. 'But I must ask you not to inform the press as His Royal Highness wishes to spend a quiet evening.'

'Of course, sir,' said the manager. 'I shall be delighted.'

He hung up and began getting ready for the evening's events. First he went to a corner store and bought a bag full of cheap glass beads which looked rather like diamonds and rubies. Then he phoned his friends who were in on the plan to tell them to arrive at his house at seven o'clock in their costumes.

The manager of Ciro's was also getting ready. Although he kept his promise not to tell the press, he told all his regular customers so that they could come to dine alongside the Crown Prince. By eight o'clock both men were prepared.

First to arrive at Ciro's were a pair of 'security guards', in reality Moran's friends. They found the restaurant packed with the smartest and richest people in Los Angeles. Movie producers rubbed shoulders with businessmen and actors. They searched the restaurant for criminals and possible assassins. Then they sent word to the 'Crown Prince' that all was well.

A huge limousine, hired for the night, pulled up at the door of Ciro's and Moran stepped out. He was dressed in full Arabian costume, complete with sandals and loose, flowing robes. In his hand he grasped a leather bag containing the cheap beads.

Acting with all the pride and haughtiness expected of royalty, he led his friends into Ciro's, occupied the best table and ordered a huge meal of the most expensive items on the menu. Lobsters, salmon and massive steaks appeared on his table, along with fine wines.

As the meal ended, he beckoned the bandleader over and muttered meaningless gibberish to the man posing as his interpreter.

'His Royal Highness would like to thank you for playing so well,' said the man.

Moran then pulled a massive 'jewel' from his bag and handed it to the bandleader with a flourish. Realising that he had everybody watching him, he then waved the bag around and poured the contents on the floor. Thinking that a fortune in jewels was there for the taking, everybody in the restaurant dived for them. Guests, musicians and waiters were all struggling and fighting over the heap of beads on the floor.

In the confusion, Moran and his friends ran from the restaurant, without paying the huge bill which they had run up. When the restaurant owners realised how they had been fooled they were furious. But later they found that the publicity the trick had caused meant that many new diners were visiting the restaurant. Soon, other restaurant owners were wanting fake celebrities at their restaurants. When Moran revealed himself, he was in great demand for evening performances.

A prank which had rather more serious results was staged by Private Snooks, a driver in the British Army during World War I. When on rear duties, his regiment was stationed in a small village near Amiens in northern France. Each night the men would walk to a small bar in the village for a drink or two. The owner of the bar, Madame Bauge, gradually became

very friendly with the company sergeant, who would make sure he was the last to leave the bar, so he could kiss Madame Bauge goodnight.

One night in March 1917, as the men were leaving the bar, they began grumbling.

'Lucky old Sarge,' said one. 'Getting a kiss goodnight and a free drink, if I know him.'

'We can't even tease him. He'd put us on a charge if we said anything.'

Snooks grinned wickedly.

'I've had an idea lads,' he chuckled.

'What is it?' they demanded.

'Never you mind,' he replied. 'Just stay here and watch.'

With that, he crept back towards the bar. Moving silently, he slid along the wall until he stood right beside the door. He heard chairs being moved around and the footsteps coming towards the door. He pushed himself flat against the wall.

The door opened, spilling light into the dark night.

'Good night, Sergeant,' whispered Madame Bauge.

'Good night, *ma chérie*,' said the Sergeant, bending forwards to kiss the woman.

Suddenly Snooks leapt forward, pushed the sergeant aside, kissed Madame Bauge and ran off into the night.

He and his friends laughed about the prank all the way back to the regimental camp. Even the sergeant thought the trick was rather amusing, but warned him not to try it again. Madame Bauge, however, did not find it funny at all. She reported Snooks to his officer, Captain Harrison, saying that he had assaulted her.

Assaulting a civilian was a very serious charge, so Captain Harrison launched a full enquiry. When he found out what had actually happened, Harrison saw the funny side. But as a complaint had been made, he had to send Snooks for trial by the regiment's colonel.

At the trial the indignant Madame Bauge described what had happened. Snooks made no attempt to deny the fact, but protested that it had only been a joke. Nonetheless he was found guilty of causing a nuisance to a civilian. He was sentenced to seven months imprisonment.

That night the Germans launched a large scale attack during which a shell struck the regimental HQ, destroying all records of the trial. Snooks, Harrison and everyone else in the regiment hoped that would be the end of it. Unfortunately the bureaucrats at Divisional HQ demanded a retrial. Once again the process of trial was begun, but by this time the Sergeant had talked Madame Bauge into dropping the charges. Snooks was a free man, but he had received a severe shock. Clearly pranks can have their price to pay!

Inspector Eustace of Scotland Yard played a trick which brought him a large reward. A London convent was suffering from a series of minor thefts. Somebody was creeping into the church at night and making off with the collection box and other valuables. Whenever a nun tried to catch the crook, he failed to show up. It was as if he were able to spot a trap.

The Inspector visited the church to investigate. First he interviewed all the nuns, then toured the buildings. His practised eye soon spotted how the thief was getting over the wall around the convent and so into the church.

Then he noticed something else. The door to the church was flanked by a pair of statues of saints dressed in flowing robes. He had an idea. He went to see the Mother Superior.

'I must ask you to help me with a little plan,' he said.

'Of course, we shall be happy to help in any way we can,' replied the Mother Superior.

'In that case,' said Eustace, 'I want you to leave the church unguarded tonight, but to lock me inside.'

The Mother Superior frowned.

'Men are not allowed in the convent after dark,' she said.

Inspector Eustace smiled. 'I realise that,' he said. 'But if you want to catch this thief you will have to let me stay.'

Eventually the Mother Superior agreed. Then he made a surprising request.

'I will also need to borrow a sheet and a box of chalk,' he said. The Mother Superior agreed to provide him with his strange equipment.

That evening he waited inside the church while the nuns left and locked him in. He told them to behave exactly as normal so that the crook would think they had gone to bed and the church was empty.

As night fell, Inspector Eustace stood beside the door. He took his normal clothes off and draped the sheet around himself. Then he took out the chalk and covered his hair, arms and legs with chalk dust. He settled down to wait.

Soon after midnight, he heard quiet footsteps

approaching the door. Then there was a slight scraping sound as a pick was inserted into the lock. He hurriedly stood beside one of the statues of the saints and raised his arms in a statue-like pose. He stood perfectly still.

The door slowly opened, and a man dressed in dark clothes slipped inside. Looking carefully around, he moved stealthily through the church. He had seen Eustace, of course, but thought he was a statue.

As he watched, the thief crept silently towards the altar. He took a silver candlestick and began to move silently back towards the door. When he was within a few paces of the door, Inspector Eustace suddenly moved forwards.

'I arrest you—' he began, but he got no further.

With an ear-splitting yell of terror, the crook leapt into the air and then crashed heavily to the ground in a dead faint. He thought that a statue had suddenly come to life.

When he recovered, he found himself handcuffed to a policeman with the Inspector, now out of his disguise, looking on.

A man who called himself Jim Candell played a nasty trick in January 1983, when he phoned the employment exchange in San Diego, California.

'Hello, sir, can I help you?' asked the clerk.

You sure can,' he replied. 'My name's Jim Candell and I run the Eagle Demolition Company and I've got a problem. I need some men.'

The clerk brightened up. He usually had people phoning in looking for work, not offering it.

'Yes, sir,' he said. 'How many did you require?'

'I reckon seventy-five should do it,' said Candell.

'But I'll only need them for one day. It's a special job, you see, and my permanent staff can't stretch to it.'

'Tomorrow,' he said. 'Tell them to turn up at 1236 Western Avenue at nine a.m. I'll pay them $40 each, but they must bring their own tools. Picks, shovels and the like. Got it?'

'I sure have,' said the clerk. 'I'll get as many men there as I can.'

'Thanks,' said Candell and rang off.

While the employment exchange clerk got busy phoning the various building labourers on his files, Candell made another phone call. This time he contacted an unemployed foreman named Robinson.

'Hello, is that Mr. Robinson?' he began.

'That's right.'

'Great,' gushed Candell. 'I've got a job for you. I want you to go to 1236 Western Avenue tomorrow and supervise a demolition job for me. None of my regular men are free tomorrow. I'll leave a job instruction and your payment on the doorstep. OK?'

'Sounds fine to me, replied Robinson.

The following morning he arrived at the address to find a bungalow which was boarded up and had not been lived in for some months. Nailed to the front door was an envelope, with his name on it, which he opened. Inside he found a $50 bill and the following letter.

Dear Mr Robinson,

Thank you for agreeing to supervise this job for me, I want you to demolish the bungalow, 1236 Western Avenue, for and on behalf of the Eagle Demoliton Company Inc.

I want the materials laid out in neat piles in the garden. Bricks in one pile, timber in the second and scrap in a third.

I shall arrive at 5 p.m. with a truck to begin removal of materials. I shall also bring with me the payment for the men.

I enclose $50 for your help in this matter.

Yours sincerely,
Jim Candell

Robinson read the note and then slipped it into his pocket. By 9 a.m. a crowd of around seventy men, all equipped with shovels, picks and crowbars, had gathered. Robinson set them to work tearing the house apart and piling the materials up in the front garden. By 4.30 p.m. the job was finished.

The men set up a small stove to make themselves coffee and sat down to wait for Candell to arrive with their money. At five, Candell had not turned up. Half an hour later he had still not arrived.

By six o'clock, when there was still no sign of Candell, Robinson got worried. He tried phoning the Employment Exchange, but they had closed for the evening. Then he asked the phone company for the number of the Eagle Demolition Company. After a pause the operator told him that no such company had a phone in San Diego.

Next he called the police. After lengthy enquiries, it turned out that there was no such company as Eagle Demolition anywhere in the state. Nor was there anyone called Jim Candell.

While the labourers, Robinson and a police officer

were discussing the matter, a car pulled up and a smartly dressed young man got out. He walked up to the property, then stopped in surprise.

'Excuse me, sir,' said the policeman. 'Are you Mr. Candell?'

'No,' replied the man. 'My name is Campbell. Where is my house?'

It turned out that the bungalow had just been bought by Campbell, with the idea of repairing it and moving in. Nobody ever discovered who 'Jim Candell' really was, nor why he would have wanted to destroy the building. Campbell could not think of any enemies he might have, so the expensive prank remains a total mystery.

Rotten Robbers

Crooks are only human and some of them have weaknesses and habits every bit as peculiar as those of more honest people. One English thief was brought to justice in 1924 by just such a habit. He loved sweets and would do anything to keep his sweet tooth satisfied.

He was a porter on the Great Western Railway. As well as drawing his pay he was in the habit of stealing crates of merchandise which were deposited at his station. The skill with which he stole crates was remarkable and he managed to make off with several packages without being suspected of anything.

One day in March a crate of goods went missing, and with it a large box of liquorice allsorts which had been lying nearby. The police were called and Detective Harris visited the scene of the crime.

'Now then,' said Harris to the stationmaster, 'when did the goods go missing?'

'This morning,' he replied. 'They were there at nine o'clock, but had gone by eleven.'

'And did you see any strangers, or anything unusual?' questioned Harris.

'No, nothing,' said the stationmaster.

The detective had a look around the station, but he could find no clues. Short of placing a policeman there to guard all the goods, there was nothing Harris could do. He knew that the cost of putting a man on guard was too high to be worthwhile and he left the station knowing that only luck could help him catch the crook.

The very next day Harris had left his home to walk to the police station when he saw a man walking in the opposite direction wearing the uniform of a railway porter, and leading a young boy by the hand.

As Harris drew level with the pair he saw that they were eating liquorice allsorts from a large box, just like the one stolen from the station the day before.

'Excuse me,' said Detective Harris, stopping the man. 'But would you mind telling me where you got those sweets from?'

Before the porter could say a word, his son chipped in, 'Dad brought them home from work,' he said, 'He often brings things home from work.'

Harris arrested the man on the spot. A quick search of his home revealed several items stolen from the railway.

Sometimes it is the honest person who is caught out by a simple trick and the crook who gains. In the seventeenth century William Davis, a highly respected farmer in Bagshot, began robbing coaches in order to pay his debts. For no less than forty-two years Davis led his double life of highwayman and farmer before being caught. His special skill was to trick people out of their money.

One day he was walking along the Exeter Road disguised as a pedlar when he came across a man who appeared to be a poor shepherd. The two men got talking.

'You know,' said Davis, 'I've heard that there are several dangerous robbers active on this road lately.'

'Yes,' said the shepherd. 'I heard that someone robbed the Exeter mail coach two weeks ago.'

Davis chuckled to himself. It was he who had held up the coach, stealing over a hundren golden guineas from the occupants. 'Really?' said Davis, pretending to be surprised. 'Is there nothing to stop these thieves?'

'Only cunning men can hope to escape the robbers,' said the shepherd knowingly.

'What do you mean?' asked Davis, hoping to learn about some new trick being employed to outwit highwaymen such as himself.

'Well,' the man went on. 'I'm not really a shepherd.'

'What?' exclaimed Davis, genuinely surprised this time. The man dressed exactly like someone who spent his life with sheep. He had a shepherd's crook and a sheep dog and even smelt of sheep.

'See,' he chuckled 'I took you in, and I fool any robbers I meet. They think a poor old shepherd isn't worth robbing and let me through. I always put on this disguise when I travel far from home. I'm really a jeweller and I carry samples of my work stitched into the lining of my cloak.' The man grinned. 'It's a good disguise, isn't it.'

'That it is,' said Davis. 'But if nobody is going to rob you, I shall have to do so myself.' He whipped out a pair of pistols and aimed them at the shocked jeweller, snapping 'Give me your cloak!'

The man handed it over and Davis ran off to where

he had left his horse. The jewels in the cloak turned out to be worth a considerable amount.

Colin Baggs of Frome in Somerset was less successful. Being rather short of money, and not too choosy about how he got hold of some, he decided to steal a car. He acquired some skeleton keys from a crooked mechanic and set out to look for a likely vehicle.

Walking down the road, he came across a Ford Sierra parked outside a house. A quick glance revealed that the driver's seat was empty. He looked around to check that nobody was watching, then turned back to the car. Using his skeleton keys, he hurriedly unlocked the door, slipped in and started the engine.

Only then did he spot the policeman sitting in the passenger seat.

Baggs was immediately arrested and found guilty of attempting to steal an unmarked police car.

Hans Fritjoff who attempted to rob a bank in Copenhagen was just as unlucky. The actual robbery went well enough, but when Fritjoff raced outside with his bag full of loot, he found that his getaway car was boxed in. Looking around in desperation, he spotted a car with an illuminated sign. Thinking it was a taxi, he flagged it down and leapt inside, only to find he had jumped into a police car.

In March 1989 a crook was arrested in Manchester for stealing from a shop till. Under questioning, he asked for several other crimes to be taken into account, including a robbery which had been puzzling police for weeks.

On the day of the crime, he had dashed into a pizza restaurant late one night. Running up to the waitress on the till, he pulled out a long knife.

'Everybody stay quiet,' he ordered, 'or the girl gets it.'

Both staff and customers watched in amazement as he then grabbed a handful of bread-sticks and dashed out.

At first police thought they were dealing with a hungry robber, but soon gave this theory up in utter bewilderment. When the crook was caught and asked to explain why he had run off with the bread-sticks, he shuffled his feet rather sheepishly.

'I thought they were rolls of banknotes,' he said.

In Southampton, in 1977, a crook entered a supermarket and put several items into a basket. When he reached the till he gave the woman on duty a ten pound note. As soon as the till drawer opened, however, he pushed her aside, seized the contents and ran off. It was later found that he had left his ten pound note behind while escaping with only £4.37!

Lucilla Desmotes, a Brazilian crook, was much more methodical. She specialised in robbing wealthy foreigners and used a method never duplicated either before or since. Before becoming a criminal, she had performed in a circus as a snake charmer. She later used her skills to rob people.

One night, she concealed several snakes about her person, then set out and called in at a smart hotel in Rio de Janiero, where she lived. Sweeping the bar with her practised eye, she picked out an expensively dressed man sitting at the bar.

Sidling up to him, she got into conversation with him; he said his name was Camino, she offered to show him the sights of Rio and he agreed and followed her outside. Now she put the second part of her plan into operation.

'Give me your money,' she whispered.

'Pardon?' asked Camino in surprise.

'You heard! Give me your money.'

He looked around in utter bewilderment, expecting to find himself threatened by men with weapons. But there was only Lucilla.

'Why should I?' he asked.

'Because of this,' said Lucilla uttering a low whistle. At the signal a well trained viper slithered from her sleeve on to his arm. He stared at the poisonous snake with distaste, but made no effort to hand over his money.

Lucilla was used to hesitant victims. She whistled again and a larger and more deadly snake crept from her other sleeve to entwine itself around Camino's arm.

'Give me your money,' she urged.

'No,' said Camino.

Lucilla was surprised, Most of her victims surrendered after two snakes were produced. But she had one more snake. Reaching into a large bag she was carrying, she produced a huge boa constrictor.

'*Give me your money*,' she repeated, waving the snake in front of Camino's face.

He sighed, took the snake from Lucilla and playfully draped it around his waist. He then grabbed her by the arms and dragged her off to a police station. She had tried her trick once too often, for Camino was a circus man himself and knew exactly how to handle snakes.

A car thief who was looking for a vehicle to steal

in south London in 1988 got more than he had bargined for. Just after dawn, when most people are asleep in their beds, he was strolling along a quiet side street, testing the doors of cars to see if they were locked.

A milkman came into sight, delivering to a block of flats. The thief waited until he was gone, then strolled over to a parked car. He pulled at the handle. It was unlocked. He was about to get in when a man leapt out of the car, pulled a gun on him and shot him in the stomach.

He was so amazed that he did not realize quite what had happened. He stared down at the blood seeping from his wound in amazement. The man who had shot him was running off down the street. Suddenly angry, he gave chase and followed the gunman to a block of flats. He then hurried to the nearest phone box and dialled the police, explaining to the officer who answered that he had just been shot.

'Shot, sir?' gasped the policeman. 'Where are you?'

The crook told him. 'I mean,' he added, 'I was only trying to pinch the chap's car. I'd expect to get hit, or even arrested, but not shot! I insist that you come and arrest him this minute!'

'We're on our way,' said the policeman.

Soon afterwards, they arrived and raided the flats into which the gunman had disappeared. They found a large supply of guns and explosives, presumably belonging to terrorists. The car thief, meanwhile, was in hosptal still fuming that someone had tried to shoot him for merely stealing a car.

In October 1922 two unknown crooks pulled off one of the most spectacular robberies in history. They broke into Scotland Yard, the famous headquarters of London's Metropolitan Police Force. Undeterred by the presence of hundreds of policemen within just metres of where they were working, the daring robbers broke through a skylight to reach the lost property office. No doubt they hoped to find several valuable items worth stealing. Unfortunately for them, the room had recently been cleared. Only two umbrellas were left. They took these and left the way they had come.

Another ambitious crook stole a credit card from a man's wallet in California in 1982. Learning how to fake the signature of the card holder, he went on a spending spree. He bought electrical items and furniture worth a fortune. Such crimes happen nearly every day. What made this theft so amazing was that the card belonged to James Bikoff, the President of the International Anti-Counterfeiting Coalition! He had no idea he had been robbed until the bills started arriving for things he had not bought.

Police in London had to deal with another counterfeiting crime when they became aware that large numbers of fake coins, made of gilded lead instead of gold, were circulating. Whoever was manufacturing the coins was obviously making a fortune. By carefully tracing the counterfeits, the police found that most of them had originated from a businessman named du Moulin.

Early one morning they moved in and arrested him. In his desk they found large quantities of fake gold coins together with forged dies for producing lead coins, and gilding equipment.

The police presented their evidence at court, building up an impressive case against du Moulin. When asked to account for what had happened, he answered simply.

'I know nothing about it.'

'What about the fake coins in your safe?' asked the prosecution lawyer.

'I did not realise they were false,' said du Moulin. 'I thought that they were genuine.'

'And the coin dies?'

'I did not know they were there.'

'Well, then what about the gilding equipment?'

'I have never seen it before in my life.'

Not surprisingly the jury was more impressed by the evidence than by du Moulin's denials. They believed he was lying and found him guilty. The judge sentenced him to a long term of imprisonment and sent him off to jail. It seemed as if yet another unremarkable criminal had been found out.

But three months later a woman named Mrs Williams demanded to see the judge who conducted the trial. Having gained admittance, the woman poured out a remarkable story

'My husband died last week,' she began.

'I am sorry to hear that,' replied the judge. Mrs Williams waved the remark aside.

'That is not why I am here,' she said. 'I am here because an innocent man is in prison and I cannot have that on my conscience.'

'I presume you mean du Moulin,' said the judge. 'I am afraid that the evidence against him was quite complete. There was no doubt as to his guilt.'

'Maybe not,' said Mrs Williams, 'but he is innocent nonetheless. My husband was an engraver, and a dishonest one at that. But we must not speak ill of the dead. The point is, he made the false coin dies which were found at du Moulin's house. But my husband did not make them for him. They were bought by his butler, Jack Peterson.'

'Peterson!' gasped the judge. 'But he gave evidence against du Moulin saying he had often seen him buying gilt.'

'Quite,' said Mrs Williams. 'He was the one forging coins. Perhaps he still is. He used to swap his fake coins for real ones belonging to du Moulin. That way his employer was the one spending the fake coins while he kept the real ones. When Peterson saw the police arrive, he stuffed the dies and gilding equipment in du Moulin's desk. I have not said anything before, because if I had done my own husband would have ended up in prison. But he is dead now and gone to a more terrible judge than yourself.'

The judge was astounded. He called a policeman at once and ordered the arrest of Peterson. When the police pounced they found fresh coin dies in his house together with new gilding equipment. He was tried, found guilty and flung into prison. Du Moulin was released and received an apology from both the police and the judge.

A man who was well-known to the police of Shropshire as a small-time burglar was seen walking home late at night with a suspiciously bulky sack. PC James stopped him.

'Good evening, Rosenthall,' said PC James. 'And where are you going at this time of night?'

'I'm on my way home from a friend's house,' he

protested 'And if you left me alone I'd get there much quicker.'

'I'm sure you would,' said PC James, 'But first show me what's in your bag.'

'It's just some stuff my mate wants cleaned.'

'Open it!'

Rosenthall did as he was instructed and revealed a collection of silver candlesticks, dishes and cruet sets. PC James eyed the silver suspiciously.

'What is your friend then?' queried PC James. 'A silversmith?'

'Yes,' said Rosenthall.

'I don't believe a word of it,' stated PC James. 'You'd better follow me down to the station.' Taking Rosenthall by the arm, the policeman hauled him off and threw him in the cells. The following morning, he checked up on the story, calling at the address where Rosenthall claimed his silversmith friend lived.

Much to their surprise the police found that the man was indeed a silversmith and had asked Rosenthall to polish up some secondhand silver he had bought. The indignant man was released and immediately walked around the corner to the offices of a solicitor named Felton.

Briefly, he outlined what had happened the previous night.

'I see,' he said. 'But if they've let you go, what do you want me to do?'

'Well,' said Rosenthall, 'I want to do the cops for wrongful arrest! Old James dragged me down to the station and locked me up for the night. My poor wife was sick with worry about me until they let me phone her to say I was OK.'

'You could have a go, but with your criminal record the police might argue that they had good suspicion to arrest you,' replied the solicitor.

'Rubbish,' said Rosenthall 'I was going about my lawful business. I want to sue them.'

'Very well,' said the solicitor, 'But you must realise that legal fees could add up to several hundred pounds. If you lost the case you would have to pay. Do you want to risk that much money?'

'Never you mind that,' said Rosenthall. 'I'll get the money.'

With that he walked out, leaving Felton to start proceedings against the police.

Eight nights later PC James was on his regular night-time beat when he saw a fat figure coming along the street towards him. As the man approached, he seemed to be trying to hide his face. Thinking this rather suspicious, the policeman stopped him.

'Excuse me, sir,' he said. 'Good heavens, it's Rosenthall!' PC James looked at the figure in front of him. He was a skinny man, yet here he was filling his coat as if he weighed several stone. The policeman was convinced that there was something suspicious, but hesitated to arrest someone already suing him for wrongful arrest. Finally, though, he went ahead and took the suspect down to the police station.

'Not again!' said the desk sergent as James led Rosenthall in.

'Yes,' said James. 'But there is definitely something fishy this time.'

'You said that last week,' reminded the sergeant. 'Still, let's get to work.'

The sergeant watched as James unbuttoned Rosenthall's coat. Underneath was a smart dress shirt, and under that a second shirt, then a smart jacket, then a silk shirt, then a second jacket, this time a tweed, and finally a cotton shirt. As James passed the garments over, the sergeant went through the pockets. They were stuffed full of watches, jewellery and other valuables.

'Where did you get this lot from then?'

Rosenthall remained silent.

'Answer the constable,' advised the sergeant.

Rosenthall still said nothing.

'Very well,' said the sergeant. 'Take him down to the cells and lock him up. We'll sort this out in the morning.'

James did as he was told and then left to return to his beat. As dawn broke he returned to the station.

'You'll like this one,' the sergeant told him. We just had a pawnbroker in here complaining someone had robbed his shop. The list of stolen jewellery and clothes exactly matches that brought in by Rosenthall. Apparently Rosenthall was trying to steal enough to pay a lawyer to sue you for wrongful arrest. I don't think you'll hear much more about that one, do you?'

PC James grinned and shook his head.

A Venezuelan burglar named Juan Gomez lived in the town of San Antonio on the border between Venezuela and Colombia. In 1976, he answered a knock on the door to find a pair of Venezuelan police on his doorstep. Realising that he was about to be arrested, he fled upstairs and rushed into his bedroom. He slammed the door shut behind him and locked it.

'Open up,' commanded one of the policemen.

'Go away,' shouted Gomez.

'If you don't open this door,' called the policeman, 'we shall kick it in.'

'You daren't,' replied Gomez. 'I am not in Venezuela anymore. I am in Columbia. You can't arrest me in this country.'

Puzzled, the policeman sent his colleague back to the police station for instructions. He found his commander and together they looked out an official map. Gomez's house actually stood right on the border between the two nations.

Meanwhile Gomez had phoned a lawyer who hurried round to explain to the police that burglary was not a crime for which people could be extradited from Colombia to Venezuela. The police left the house, but set a guard outside in case Gomez left by the front door.

Instead, though, he climbed out of the bedroom window and fled into Colombia.

Reverend Edgar Dodson was a preacher in Arkansas. He was a well respected member of the local community and his services were usually well attended. One Sunday, after a series of local robberies and burglaries, Dodson decided to preach a sermon on the wickedness of stealing.

He began by reading the Ten Commandments, laying special emphasis on 'Thou shalt not steal'. For a full twenty minutes Dodson thundered about the evils of theft. He told his congregation how they should obey the laws of the state and not commit such evil acts.

After the service, Dodson walked outside to find somebody had stolen his car.